"This book is a chance for people to benefit from the humanity and wisdom Matt Del Negro has acquired by grinding through his own *10,000 NOs* for so long. His value far exceeds his art. His talent is only outweighed by his humility and ability to connect with others and make them feel better about their own journey."

—Bedros Keuilian, CEO, FitBody Bootcamp, bestselling author, *Man Up*

"Being told 'no' can either define you or ignite you. Matt's powerful book gives you the courage and confidence to turn that devastating 'no' into inspiration. Through his resilience, determination, and breathtaking honesty, Matt shows how to navigate the sting of rejection and convert it into the satisfaction of success! This book is a serious life changer!"

—Sue Hollis, Cofounder, The TravelEdge Group, Coach, Adventurepreneur, Top 10 Women Entrepreneurs in Australia, author of *Riding Raw: A Journey from Empty to Full*, motorbike racer

"If you want a reality check, a connection to what it takes to get where you want to go in life . . . advice about the reality of getting past *10,000 NOs* to the one 'Yes' you desire and will commit to, then make this your Life Bible. Absorb it. Listen to the words. Then go no further. Settle in. And make Matt's experience . . . yours."

—Roger Fishman, Adventure Photographer, author, *What I Know*, former Head of Marketing, CAA

MATTHEW **DEL NEGRO**

10,000 NOs

HOW TO
OVERCOME
REJECTION
ON THE WAY
TO YOUR
YES

WILEY

Deirdre, for standing by when the "no"s felt heaviest
Donovan and Bronwyn, may you never let the critic count
Everyone else, for helping and encouraging me to keep going

Contents

Introduction   *ix*

Chapter 1   Getting Started   1

Chapter 2   Work Ethic   13

Chapter 3   Performance, Anxiety, and Instinct   25

Chapter 4   Discipline and Training   41

Chapter 5   Risk   53

Chapter 6   Perseverance   65

Chapter 7   Reframing   77

Chapter 8   Surrender   89

Chapter 9   Transformation   103

Chapter 10 Leadership   117

Chapter 11 Meditation and Relaxation   133

Chapter 12 Belief and Faith   147

Chapter 13 The Subconscious   159

Chapter 14   Just Be a Good Person   169

Chapter 15   Focus and Singularity   177

Chapter 16   Facade versus Reality   189

Epilogue   197

Acknowledgments   201

About the Author   203

Index   205

Introduction

I had coffee recently with a very successful documentary filmmaker friend. The feature documentary he made a few years ago won the Sundance Film Festival documentary competition and sold for a lot of money. The next one he made was also quite lucrative, which is no easy feat for a documentary film. His most recent film, however, did not immediately find worldwide distribution the way the others had, so he reached out to me to share the news and talk through his frustrated feelings on the matter. When I realized the intent of his coffee meeting request I said, "Wow, I guess I really *am* a Rejection Expert, huh?" He laughed before explaining that he hadn't called me because of my own punishing track record. It was just that his very supportive wife, who is not in our industry, did not have the comparable experience of seeing two years of work deflate in front of her eyes due to the changing tides of opinion. And his fellow documentary filmmaker friends were somewhat in competition with him, so they might not completely commiserate. It was at this point that I fully realized the need for this book.

This book will change you as much as you let it. It will not "solve" your life or tell you how to turn every "no" into a "yes." But it *will* crack open more questions and deepen your quest for success if you allow it. It does not contain magic, just truth. It sheds light on many of the principles so many of us have pondered for years: perseverance, performance, work ethic, risk, belief, hope, faith. I focus the chapters in this book on these principles as well as on getting started, instinct, discipline and training, reframing, surrender, transformation, leadership, meditation and relaxation, the subconscious, being a good person, and facade versus reality. Some topics and chapters overlap as they are interrelated, and all present real-world perspectives. You can devour it in one sitting, as an actor's entertaining albeit sometimes cringe-worthy memoir, or jump around willy-nilly when inspiration and curiosity beckon you, using it more like a self-development manifesto. Either way, I hope that it will make you laugh, inspire you, and encourage you to take one more step toward whatever it is that brings fulfillment for you and makes your life feel well spent.

Author Malcolm Gladwell proposed that people only become experts in a field after they've dedicated themselves to it for 10,000 hours. I agree with him. But I've also pondered the ability and practice of withstanding the word "no." What defines my career, or anyone's for that matter, is the way I have chosen to react to constant rejection, perceived failures, and "lucky breaks" that have fallen apart due to forces outside of my control. That type of reaction, both when it was admirable and when it was embarrassingly petty, is what most people would call attitude, outlook, or perspective. For all of us, our ability to persevere is derived from a combination of innate instincts embedded deep in our DNA and lessons from the major influences and influenc*ers* in our lives, including our parents, teachers, coaches, bosses, friends, siblings and so many others. It is our *choice* to seek out others who strengthen our resilience, as well as situations that test it, or to gravitate toward smaller-minded people who wish to keep us where *they* are or where they think we should be rather than encouraging our growth and challenging their own self-imposed limits.

In July 2017, after racking up over two decades' worth of rejections, I launched a podcast, *10,000 NOs*, in an attempt to find out how men and women in every field imaginable, facing seemingly insurmountable obstacles, overcame their "no"s. What followed in the next three years has become the education of my life. This book contains quotes from some of my podcast guests that so perfectly reinforce the principles I have learned mostly through trial and error. Some of those guests are famous, some are not; two has died since our conversation and most are thriving. But the common thread is that each and every one of them is as flawed and as full of contradictions, pain, sadness, worry, joy, laughter, sorrow, and victory as the rest of us. They are human. They do not possess "the answers" nor were they born on the Island of "Yes." All of them have stumbled upon the same tough truths by grappling with, battling, and overcoming a mountain of "no"s. It's not just a matter of learning from the tough times we experience, but *what* we learn, *why* it's important to learn from it, *when* we learn it—from hours to years after—and *how* we use those lessons to persevere.

No matter who you are, or where you are in your career, you will have setbacks. You will be in need of counsel from friends and other supporters. And no book or piece of advice will make your pain go away immediately. There is no magic pill. But knowing that others have suffered in ways similar to you and somehow made it through is enough to help you pick up the pieces, reflect on them, and move on. Ironically, when I sat down with my documentary filmmaker friend I was feeling particularly terrible and self-judgmental about this book. That was when he told me about the Five Stages of Creativity, which somehow, I had never heard before:

Stage 1 - I'm really excited about this.

Stage 2 - This isn't as good as I thought it was.

Stage 3 - This is terrible.

Stage 4 - This is actually better than I realized.

Stage 5 - I'm really excited about this.

If everything were easy all the time, you would not value that ease. If "yes" were the answer to your every wish and demand, every victory and windfall would be meaningless. You *think* you want comfort, but what you really need is *progress*. Progress only arrives when a struggle is overcome. So, while I wish I could send you off into the world telling all your friends that this book solved everything for you, I know that would be unrealistic. Instead, I send you off into the world urging you to lean into your 10,000 "no"s. I urge you to really feel their pain and let that pain guide you past the "no" to greener pastures. I urge you to learn from them what *not* to do the next time, so you can turn those "no"s into a "yes." I urge you to be grateful for them, for in them lies the wisdom of humanity and experience. There is no greater teacher than that which reminds you that your salvation lies in always striving, until your last dying breath.

Matthew Del Negro
January 2020

1

Getting Started

"You never know when those other supportive factors are going to want to converge around your work, but they won't if you don't take the first step."

—*Jessica Blank, Writer*, The Exonerated

There are many things that can muddy the waters and make something so simple, like trying a new hobby or ditching a bad habit, seem complex. As crazy as it sounds, most humans will come up with excuse after excuse to try to wiggle out of doing the one thing they know they *need* to do in order to accomplish their deepest desires. But really, it all begins with one step. I believe you will only take that step, and change the course you are on, when the thought of *not* doing something becomes more painful to you than the thought of giving it a try. It really is that simple.

Keep It Simple, Stupid

The truth that most people fail to acknowledge, however, is that doing something, even if you're following a dream, can still be painful a lot of the time. When you're following a dream, though, there's a pot of gold at the end of the pain. That pot may not be filled with literal gold, but it should at least hold the gold of *fulfillment*. That fulfillment usually comes in the form of peace, satisfaction, and a pride that only comes from living with purpose.

> "We don't tell ourselves, 'I'm never going to write my symphony.' Instead we say, 'I'm going to write my symphony; I'm just going to start tomorrow.'"
>
> —*Stephen Pressfield*, The War of Art

People these days, myself included, are obsessed with the origin stories of those who have broken away from the pack to take the road less traveled. This is not surprising given the difficulty required to take the first step down *any* path. The question I'm asked the most, besides how I memorize all my lines, is how I became a professional actor. The trite answer I usually give in interviews is that it started with a girl. That leads to a story about a breakup in college while studying abroad, which ultimately led to my decision to quit playing lacrosse my junior year at Boston College. Then, seemingly out of nowhere, I auditioned for a play, and the rest is history. But perhaps a more truthful and accurate answer is that it started with a plethora of proverbial "no"s throughout my childhood.

Before You Take Your First Step, Ask Yourself Why You're Moving

Most people can trace their *why* back to some pain, rejection, or perceived loss in childhood that they are now trying to fix.

I am no different. For me, my *why* was forged in the pain of my parents' marriage, which looked one way to my immediate family and another to the rest of the world. As the youngest member of the family, and the peacekeeper, I was constantly interpreting one family member's actions to another. Socially, my role was similar. I could always relate to most people so I'd find myself explaining one person to another, even if they were part of vastly different social subsets. The price I paid for keeping the peace was that I internalized everything and carried it around with me. Looking back now, it is easier to see that my career choice did not really come out of nowhere, the way I previously viewed it, as my job now is to interpret the words of writers and the experiences of the characters I play. But I had zero awareness of this link back then.

On top of carrying other people's secrets around, as well as my own pain and frustration, I could never to seem to attain the things I wanted the most. As far back as the fifth grade, I'd pursue a girl I liked, get close to her, and muster up the courage to ask her out. But, one way or another, I'd end up alone after it fell apart due to a change of heart or some other obstacle I never saw coming until it was too late. Rejection is defined as the dismissing of an idea or the spurning of a person's affections, and I had plenty of both. I feel bad for a certain girl I "loved" in fifth grade because, while I've only run into her on rare occasions since we graduated high school, I never miss the opportunity to remind her of our date that never happened. I had charmed her enough to eventually elicit a "yes" when I asked her to the year-end town carnival, but on the night of the event, she stood me up. Two friends of mine still love to laugh about the memory of me riding The Whip alone in the rain. And while I can laugh at myself about it now, back then it added to the feeling that I was not where I wanted to be emotionally, and not sure I'd ever get there.

While I was not a child actor, I still managed to get a "no" when I auditioned for the role of the Cowardly Lion in an elementary school production of *The Wizard of Oz*. I had forgotten this story for a long time because it occurred long before I thought of acting as a viable career. It's only been in recent years, as I've reflected about the lessons I've learned in the course of my career, that I've remembered it. It was a play in which the kids in my class were *required* to participate. I really thought I could get the role of the Cowardly Lion until the new girl, upon whom I had a massive crush, completely outshined me with her audition. (Side note: this was a different crush. I moved on from the carnival stander-upper. But I screwed this one up, too—it wasn't until eighth or ninth grade, when I admitted to liking her three years prior, that she revealed *she* had a crush on *me* when she first moved to our school. Talk about missed opportunities. More on self-dispensed "no"s later.)

In the present day, I motivate myself by the thought that there is always someone out there more talented than me ready to take my roles. Perhaps it started back then, with my grade-school crush. She could sing and dance, and she had what people might call "it." My talent, on the other hand, was rewarded with the consolation prize of playing Uncle Henry. I still remember my sole line, telling Auntie Em I had to fix the incubator. It was an illustrious beginning to my career, I assure you. This "no" was thrown onto the ever-increasing pile of rejections, but I didn't think much of it, at least consciously, because I didn't care about acting back then.

Sports, on the other hand, felt like my life when I was growing up. Unfortunately, my desire to be good at them was not matched by my talent. I'd work my butt off obsessively only to remain skinny, weak, and slow. The fact that I made it as far as I did in athletics is a sheer reflection of a burning desire in me to be accepted and valued. On my own, despite the many things I had going for me and the many great friends and family members who surrounded me, I largely felt like I was not enough.

No matter which "no" I credit as the origin of my career, it was somehow forged in the pain of rejection and the desire to overcome it.

Obviously, all of those childhood "no"s didn't kill me and neither did the "no" of my emotionally harrowing experience in Italy over the summer of 1992. Perhaps the expression "That which does not kill you will make you stronger" is popular because it reflects a truth. The breakup in Italy is what forced me to dig deeper and find something more fully satisfying than being a member of my college lacrosse team. Confusing feelings had been percolating inside me prior to my trip to Italy, inducing a full-blown panic attack long before I had ever heard that term. But, like many people, rather than examine the origins of my unrest, I chose to ignore my anxiety because I was too scared to take the first step.

On the surface, things were looking good for me by the spring of my sophomore year in Chestnut Hill. I had a beautiful girlfriend, a spot on the varsity team, grades that kept me on the Dean's List, and a lot of friends. But beneath the surface lurked a different story. Despite the fact that I thought I was in love for the first time, the panic attacks were brought on by the fact that I had been questioning the relationship subconsciously. I was just too scared to do anything to jeopardize it because I thought it was everything I wanted. There was a chasm deep within me that I had been avoiding and it created a gap between my inner self and the facade I presented to the world. That facade began to crumble in Italy when my girlfriend had the courage to do what I had feared by breaking off our relationship.

The truth inside me rose up, grabbed me by the throat, and got my attention. Uncharacteristically, I skipped out of all the classes I was supposed to be taking and, instead, found a patch of grass in front of a small church in Perugia where I dumped all of my jagged thoughts into the journal my sister had given to me prior to my trip. It was as though there was an angry artist inside of me, no longer allowing me to put a muzzle on him, writing it. He told me that I couldn't continue to go down the path upon which I was traveling. It was an exhilarating yet frightening experience. That journal contains the first traces of my desire to act and write. I look back on this period as fortunate now, but it is no exaggeration to say that, at the time, I feared I was going to die in Italy with no friends or family around to witness it.

> "I went back to my room, pulled my pistol out and put it in my mouth and was getting ready to blow my head off. Thankfully, I had a picture of my wife and kids on the desk across from me. I saw that as I was sitting there with a gun in my mouth and thought, 'What're you doing?' So I put my gun away and I went and sought help for the first time. And I'd love to say that I woke up. I didn't. I stayed on the X for a while. I still played the victim. I tried to convince myself, 'You're being thrown under the bus. You're doing the right thing.' But it literally took me about five months. I hadn't hit rock bottom yet."
>
> *Jason Redman, Retired Navy SEAL,*
> New York Times *Best-Selling Author*

The result of this breakdown/breakthrough was that the following spring at Boston College, after a brief period of going back to lacrosse and the beaten path I had traveled for so long, I quit the team, stepped out of my comfort zone, and auditioned for a play. After losing out to my roommate, who was also auditioning for the first time, I gave it another shot and scored the lead in a one-act play. It was performed in a lecture hall, rather than an actual theater. But despite the humble venue, I enjoyed the experience so much that I told anyone who would listen that

I was going to be an actor. While this may sound dramatic and grand, over a year later, after that one-act play, I had not done any more plays.

Upon graduating, I moved back home with the plan to save enough money to move to New York City and pursue a career in acting. I had taken an acting class my senior year and added a Film Studies minor to my English Literature major, but I had not acted aside from that lecture-hall production. On top of this, after 27 years of marriage, my parents decided to split that summer, so moving back into the house where I grew up without my Dad living there was an adjustment. There were many thoughts swimming through my head, but the primary one was how I could turn my new dream into a reality.

There is no standard how-to manual containing a list of the first steps in becoming an actor, because the *how* is unique for each individual. Classes can be attended, mentors can be sought out, and the skills required to excel can be attained through training. But the *why* is the fuel that will propel you. A strong *why* will obliterate all of the inevitable blockades and barriers you will undoubtedly face no matter *what* field you choose. If your *why* is not aligned with your innermost joy and your biggest dreams, you *may* find success, but eventually you will experience some version of the breakdown I had in Italy. It may not crumble your life or turn you 180 degrees the way it did me. It may not cause you panic attacks. But there will be cracks in your facade. Eventually, if you're not careful, you'll look back wondering whose life you lived.

"I drove a cab for years, I proofread in law firms, I worked in a factory when I kind of dropped it all out and went out to Colorado. I cleaned Greyhound buses on Eleventh Avenue from eleven at night 'til seven in the morning in summers while I went to school.

No, I didn't start making a living for real until my son was born."
—*Richard Schiff, Actor, Emmy Award Winner,*
The West Wing

That experience in Italy, when everything bubbled out of me, made me certain that I wanted to pursue something that required *all* of my faculties. I wanted to somehow relieve the knot of emotions and unfulfilled desires tangled in my gut. Thus, my *why* was a desire to express myself psychologically, spiritually, physically, and mentally and the way I guessed I could do that was through acting. But just because I'd found my *why*, did not mean I knew exactly *how* to start.

Everybody Needs Some Billy Sometimes

The challenge for me to begin my pursuit as an actor was that I had almost no experience. Everyone needs to start somewhere and I was no different. The pain of *not acting*, for me, outweighed the fear of falling on my face in front of others. I wanted to start as soon as possible, so I scanned a local paper and found a casting notice. A community theater a few towns over from where I grew up was doing the musical *The Mystery of Edwin Drood*. The audition required each hopeful actor to sing 16 bars of music, accompanied by a pianist. I called the phone number and admitted that I didn't have 16 bars of music to sing. I explained that I could play a little piano, even less guitar, and I could carry a tune. When I asked if it would it be okay if I just "sang some Billy Joel" there was a long pause. After what felt like an eternity, I heard, "Sure. Just bring the sheet music."

The following week I drove over to the theater after a full day of my summer job laying patios with a mason. I'd had time to shower and change, but my choice of wardrobe was hardly appropriate for a musical set in the 1860s. I entered the theater in jeans, a white t-shirt, and a pair of beaten up, low-cut Converse Chuck Taylors. To say I stuck out like a sore thumb would be an understatement. I looked like I was headed to a frat party while the rest of the hopeful actors wore some semblance of period garb similar to the setting of the musical. The way the audition was set up—which I have never experienced since—was that every person who went up on stage to sing did so in front of everyone else waiting to go. Once you were done, you were free to leave. Suddenly, I wished that I had showed up late so there would be no one else to watch this potential debacle, but I hid my insecurity and sat seemingly confidently in the back of the theater waiting for my turn. Heart pounding underneath my increasingly sweaty t-shirt, I began to coach myself. Running through a list of things I'd accomplished up until this point in my life in a desperate attempt to quell my nerves and convince myself this was nothing I couldn't handle, I began to find my confidence.

This lasted until the first girl got up on stage. She was beautiful and blonde, a few years younger than me, but she appeared older because of her formal period wardrobe and the way she carried herself. She handed her sheet music to the pianist as though she'd done this a million times before. The pianist began to play. When this young woman began to belt out her tune, all my insecurities came rushing back. She was amazing. I sat questioning my decision to volunteer for this torture and wondered why I thought *I* deserved to be here. Somehow, by the time her 16 bars came to an end, I had convinced myself that she was just a fluke. I told myself the rest of the auditionees would be normal, like me.

This theory crashed to the ground when the next person was called to the stage. This young man, dressed appropriately in a suit, was also classically trained. He had the kind of voice you hear on Broadway, and as his song hit its climax, I realized they might all be like this. That realization proved to be true when the next three or four actors, even those who were considerably younger than me, blew the doors off the place. I was looking around for the exit and thinking about sneaking out when my name was called.

Oh boy, I thought, here comes the moment of truth.

I walked up to the front of the theater, feeling all eyes on me. Hopping onto the stage as casually as I could, I thought if I wasn't the most classically trained, I was at least going to appear the most confident. Fake it 'til you make it, son. When I hit the stage, something shifted inside me. I remembered why I was there. I might not be classically trained, but I loved to perform. I remembered my plan to stick out by *embracing* the fact that I was different. I walked to the center and planted my feet. The pianist asked for my sheet music and I stared back. Mustering all the confidence and courage I could, I told him I'd be singing a cappella. The sheer audacity of it, knowing I was outclassed but forging ahead anyway, was like a rush of adrenaline. After taking a deep breath and exhaling, I began snapping my fingers and tapping my foot. I fell back on what I knew: Billy Joel.

While I didn't have much real stage experience, I *did* spend many a day and night in junior high and high school, sometimes with friends, sometimes alone, playing piano and singing. Somewhere inside me was a performer dying to get out and all he needed was for me to take this first step and give him the opportunity. I was alive. Whereas just minutes before the attention had nearly crumbled me, as I sang now, I felt everyone's eyes on me and I *liked* it. I was where I was supposed to be. And even though the odds that they'd think I was right for *this* play were slim to none, I didn't care. I had taken the leap and I'd be right for something, *some*day.

In a beautiful twist of fate, my courage was rewarded and I was offered a role. And not a small role, either. I was the Chairman. *The Mystery of Edwin Drood* is a play within a play, so prior to the curtain going up they needed someone to improvise with audience members as they entered the theater, in a British accent, no less. Breaking the fourth wall of the theater and speaking directly to the audience throughout the play, the Chairman was to introduce the play, narrate it, and jump into the action as Mayor Sapsea for several songs and scenes. He was one of the leads and I had the time of my life.

At the end of the run, the director pulled me aside and told me she had worried about finding the right person to play the Chairman because it required different skills than any of the other roles. When I had hopped on stage in jeans and a t-shirt and started snapping my fingers, she knew immediately that I was her guy. My differences, the very thing I feared would embarrass me, were the reason I got the gig. But I never would have learned that if I hadn't taken the first step to get started.

Too many people I speak with get in their own way because they're judging themselves as if they're at the finish line even though the starting gun has barely sounded. Rome wasn't built in a day, and neither was any good business, physique, or skyscraper. Things take time to grow, and usually that timetable is *a lot* slower than you hope for it to be. Self-judgment and crippling self-criticism are *not* the path to your goal. There are many paths to success, depending on who you are and what you want to do. Those paths are as varied and different as the number of people in the world, but they share one thing in common: each one begins with a first step.

Top Three Takeaways

1. Before starting something new, remind yourself that "failure is built into the game."

2. You don't need to know *how* to do something. Often the things that people *think* make them qualified for a job or a calling are not really the deciding factor anyway. The most important factor is *why* you are chasing this goal in the first place.

3. If *you* say "no" to yourself, you never give *them* the chance to say "yes." *They* usually don't know what they need anyway, until they see it.

CHAPTER

2

Work Ethic

"If the best guy, the most talented guy, who could make it just on their talent, has the work ethic of someone with no talent, that's scary. And that's Prince. And that's Michael Jackson."

—Jimmy Jam, Music Producer
Producer of the Year 1987
Most nominations for Producer of the Year

If you watch even just a few interviews with celebrities and sports legends, you're bound to uncover one of the great contradictions of the motivational world: that *everyone* who has risen to the top of their field claims to be "the hardest worker in the room." From Dwayne "The Rock" Johnson to Will Smith to Ultimate Fighting Champion Conor McGregor, every one of them will tell you, "I'll die before I'm outworked." Well, for the sake of our culture and entertainment, let's hope all three of them are never

13

training in the same room. All kidding aside, the point is that, for *anyone* who wants to make a major impact along the lines of Oprah, Mother Theresa, or that incredible kindergarten teacher at your child's school, a strong work ethic is required.

Nature versus Nurture

While there are many areas in my life where I do not feel naturally gifted, I was blessed with a relatively strong work ethic right out of the womb. Some of my earliest memories involve a fascination with chipping away at a task or skill in order to reach a goal that was not within my immediate grasp. This is not to say that I didn't enjoy lying around watching movies or daydreaming as a child, but I'm guessing that if you asked anyone who has known me throughout the various stages of my life, they'd bring up my work ethic pretty early in the conversation. Not only did my work ethic feel like it was in the fabric of my DNA, it was also honed by parents who were first-generation Americans and grandparents who told me stories of making the transition from Italy to the United States and then weathering the Great Depression. There were so many stories about sacrificing *now* in order to benefit *later* that somehow it all seeped into my subconscious.

Friend and former *10,000 NOs* podcast guest Bedros Keuilian coined the term "the immigrant edge" to describe how his humble roots give him an advantage now. His father risked a lot to get the Keuilian family out from under Soviet rule to the freedom of the United States. But just being in America did not mean their troubles were gone. When he was young, Keuilian would be hoisted up into dumpsters behind grocery stores by his father to scrounge for food that had been thrown away after its official expiration date. He credits his success as an entrepreneur to his identification with the honey badger, an animal known for its ability to work feverishly and single-mindedly in pursuit of food and whatever else it needs. Those qualities, he says, came from growing up with less than everyone around him and having parents who taught him the value of hard work.

If you did not have that kind of influence, the good news is that work ethic can be learned, trained, and coaxed out of its dark cave if you have the right piece of meat to lure it. This point may be best illustrated by *10,000 NOs* guest Terry Knickerbocker's journey. Knickerbocker, an acting teacher with his own studio in Brooklyn, New York, is known for guiding actors like Sam Rockwell into Oscar-winning performances. The signature quality cited by Knickerbocker's students, clients, and employees is his incredibly detailed and dedicated work ethic. But earlier in his life, he was a self-described underachiever who would get high all the time beginning in the ninth grade. His appetite for work was only whetted when he discovered his passion for acting. He began to get roles, but soon realized his raw talent would only take him so far.

> "I didn't know what the hell I was doing, but I kept on getting these parts. I realized I reached a plateau here and I needed to train."
>
> —*Terry Knickerbocker, Acting Coach*

Prior to being considered one of the best acting coaches in a highly competitive industry, Knickerbocker failed out of Boston University. It was not a lack of ability or intelligence that cut his undergraduate studies short. It was a failure to show up to class that undid him. Regardless of the size of your talent or your natural-born abilities, if you fail to work hard or to do so consistently, you will never reach your potential. You may get by. You may even excel in comparison to your competition. But you will never be able to look yourself in the eye with the pride that comes from knowing you gave it your all.

> "You can be like Jack Horner and chisel a plum
> And think you're a wonderful guy.
> But the Man in the Glass says you're only a bum
> If you can't look him square in the eye."
>
> —"The Guy in the Glass," *Dale Wimbrow*

Passion and interest certainly play a part in consistently chipping away at a goal for long periods of time. But something that I think may be overlooked by many, which is the key to increasing a strong work ethic, is the *mindset* that usually accompanies this process. Contrary to what many people may believe, almost every high achiever known for their incredible work ethic developed it because a voice inside their head told them that their God-given talent on its own was not good enough to get them to where they wanted to be.

> "We are not particularly well-spoken, we are not particularly good-looking, we are not particularly intelligent, we are ... generally speaking a B-minus across the board, and yet we just fucking killed ourselves, and worked our asses off and found a way to push that boulder up the mountain. And I think people look at us, and rightfully so, and they think, 'If those guys can do it, I think anybody can do this.'"
>
> —*Mark Duplass, Filmmaker and Actor, on the massive success he and his brother have had in Hollywood circumnavigating the system*

The fact that these people have accomplished so much, and are many times rewarded with prestigious accolades or larger-than-average financial rewards, has caused others to incorrectly deduce that these people were just born "better than the rest of us." Someone watching a highlight reel of NBA star Steph Curry draining three-pointer buzzer-beaters in high-pressure games might think he's just a more naturally gifted shooter than the majority of his basketball counterparts. While he does possess an enormous amount of athletic ability, the painstaking detail and consistency that goes into his daily shooting regimen is well-known and something he often speaks about. A similar narrative carries across all industries, whether we are talking about an athlete, actor, comedian, CEO, or politician. These superstars' work ethics are their common thread, like an insurance policy against chance and mere talent.

Getting to Know Fear

Let's break down the psychology of a strong work ethic. Bumper stickers abound spouting slogans like "No Fear." But perhaps my friend and former podcast guest Tony Blauer has it more accurate with his own company, Know Fear. Blauer is one of the world's top self-defense experts, having trained scores of Tier One Operators (a.k.a. Navy SEALs, Army Rangers, etc.) as well as housewives and everyday citizens. His philosophy is that, rather than stick our heads in the sand pretending we are safe, we need to familiarize ourselves with fear. We need to be incredibly aware of our surroundings and the potential for danger at any time, whether it be from an assailant on the street or a car in an oncoming traffic lane. Blauer teaches that it is only in leaning into the fear and sadness of losing one's loved ones that people are motivated to take the proper precautions to reduce the chances of that happening. Fear, in this case, becomes the motivator that signs us up to get the training necessary to protect ourselves and our families. That training and awareness can be considered "good work ethic" within the realm of self-defense.

As an actor, I know fear every time I'm on a new set in a new role. My consistent training has reduced this fear. And over time, my experience has provided me examples that I can draw from, of times where I have overcome my fear in the past, which helps me to keep it in check. But new environments can bring new challenges that sometimes make me feel like I'm starting all over again. When I was young and I'd hear a legendary actor like Gene Hackman wonder if he was ever going to work again once he wrapped a film, I thought it was an insincere ploy for sympathy. But now, as a consistently working actor myself, I finally understand his statement. The years have taught me that I can never predict what is coming next. Likewise, on a new set with new players and material, a fear that I won't have what it takes to hack it can sometimes creep into my psyche. My specific career, where much of my work has consisted of extended stints on other people's shows, has brought this challenge up for me repeatedly.

The West Wing Experience

One of these intimidating stints was on *The West Wing*. While I was eventually cast as Bram Howard, the advance man of Jimmy Smits's Matt Santos character, toward the end of season 6, I had auditioned for a different role two years prior. For that audition, I had made it far enough to eventually read with the show's creator, Aaron Sorkin. Despite having had a nice run on *The Sopranos* a few years before this, I was a bit scared. The tip from the casting director before I walked into the room was that Sorkin liked it fast, so I would need to pick up my cues and keep the pace at a fast clip. While I wouldn't have considered myself a loyal fan of

The West Wing at the time, I had seen enough episodes to know that virtually every character was hyper-articulate and prone to slinging polysyllabic political jargon while marching through the maze-like halls of the West Wing or hotel corridors at a brisk pace—these "walk and talks" quickly became a hallmark of the show and a feature used by many shows since. It was intimidating, to say the least.

On top of this, while I consider myself to be an intelligent human, I have never been particularly astute when it comes to politics. With an exorbitant amount of preparation, however, I was able to successfully make it through my reading with Sorkin. Knowing that there were only a few other actors in the running, coupled with the fact that they were looking to "cast an unknown" in this role, I actually walked out of that room believing I had a legitimate shot. I was wrong. Rather than offering the role to me or one of the other handful of "unknowns," they gave it to Matthew Perry, who was fresh off of the smash hit *Friends*. Such is Hollywood. I was forced to chalk it up as another of my 10,000 "no"s when Perry eventually won an Emmy for his performance.

Two years later, in 2005, while temporarily in Los Angeles attempting to score a series regular role on a new show during pilot season (the time of year when pilots, a.k.a. first episodes of a new series, are being cast for the following season of TV), I went in again for what was advertised as a one-off guest star role on *The West Wing*. Again, there was a mountain of political jargon to climb, and my fear of flubbing it helped me to prepare for the audition enough that I was eventually chosen for the role. Ironically, I remember feeling worse coming out of that room than I did after the Sorkin audition two years before. (How an actor feels about their audition does not always correlate to whether or not they get the job.)

Getting the gig was a victory considering the pedigree of the show. But when I went to my first fitting, I picked up an inside scoop from a member of the wardrobe department, who eventually became a friend, that raised the stakes for me considerably. He told me that my storyline was part of a new direction on the show that involved the campaign trail for Jimmy Smits's character, Matt Santos, running for President. John Wells, who had since taken the reins of the show from Aaron Sorkin, was apparently using these guest spots as a way to audition actors for a potentially longer stint on the show. In essence, my new confidante was telling me, "Don't eff it up!"

Nobody Walks on the Hill!

John Hurley, my freshman football coach, ended the first practice of our ninth grade season by surprising the team with an order to take a lap around a tree that was perched atop a very steep hill that sloped down to our practice field. Mistakenly assuming we were done caused me to get a late jump on the run and, having hustled my butt off for the previous two hours, I struggled and came in almost dead last. I specifically remember thinking that maybe I wasn't cut out for this level of play and eighth grade football was my limit. But I stuck it out, stayed around, and had a good season. Building on that freshman year, I had three more good seasons, playing through the end of high school. I also quickly learned Coach Hurley's most famous catchphrase, "Nobody walks on the hill!" He was referring to that steep hill we had to climb after that first practice. *Every* time we ascended it, from that first practice on, it was drilled into our heads that we could not walk it. Instead, no matter how tired we might be, we had to sprint up.

"Nobody walks on the hill!" is a mantra I still use with my kids to this day. In fact, I use it myself for everything from motivation in the gym to prep work for roles to my overall daily hustle. It was front of my mind my first day on *The West Wing*, when I was called to set. They were finishing a scene in a school class-room before we moved on to my first scene. That's where I first met Bradley Whitford. I had seen his work on the show, and his combination of flawless machine-gun-fire dialogue combined with his loose-as-a-goose vibe was frighteningly good. I was also aware at this point that he had won an Emmy Award, among many other accolades, for his portrayal of Josh Lyman. On top of this, I was aware that all of my scenes in this episode consisted of *me* leading the charge down hallways. My character was driving the action and dialogue while flanked by actors whose work I knew, who had also been on the show far longer than me: Whitford, Smits, Teri Polo, and Janeane Garofalo, among others.

But that fear, of being the guy who comes in and turns out to be the fly in the ointment, actually saved me. Knowing that preparation and work ethic were my best weapons against the nerves associated with a high-stakes gig, I threw myself into the prep as soon as I was cast. With limited time for the in-depth research that I'd eventually do, I ran the scenes over and over, drilling the lines frontward, backward, and sideways. I'd run the scenes while I was driving, at the gym, walking around ... in an Irish accent, a Southern accent ... anything I could do so that I didn't have to *think* about lines at all once we got rolling. I thought about my character's relationship to the candidate, Matt Santos, and to the other characters as well as to the campaign itself. On my first day on the show, and all through that episode, "La Palabra," I never faltered. I was prepared, but not overconfident. Other actors, even ones I admired so much, had moments that caused us to have to cut, but I did not.

To be clear, acting is *not* about memorizing your lines. In my opinion, the best acting takes place *between* the lines. Great acting is great listening. And there are many times when, as long as you're exploring during a take, you can go up on your lines and have to stop the scene and still have usable material in that take. But an actor is usually only allowed that freedom once they are known, trusted, and have proven themselves to the director and other actors. When you're a rookie on the set, you do not want to be that person, particularly on a show that involves long and winding walk-and-talks with a Steadicam. While there was not much particularly emotional heavy lifting required of me in that first episode, my work ethic helped me prove to them that I might be an asset to the cast.

I was asked back to *The West Wing* two episodes later in the season 6 finale, and invited to the end-of-year wrap party. As I was leaving the party to head back to the East Coast, Executive Producer and Director Alex Graves said, "We'll see you at the end of the summer." I said, "Can you put that in writing?" They called my reps over the summer, guaranteeing me three out of the first five episodes in season 7, and that led to me being a significant player in what turned out to be the show's last season. I stuck around all the way through the series finale, in which my character got his own office in the West Wing.

My talent helped me in my *West Wing* experience, but I credit most of that run to my work ethic. I also credit my belief in Coach Hurley's mantra, "Nobody walks on the hill!" My healthy dose of fear, which served as a motivator, was also key. *The West Wing* material I was given did not exactly allow me to truly stretch my acting muscles. But, much like my time on *The Sopranos*, which you'll hear about in another chapter, it continues to help me score jobs to this day because it was such a high-pedigree and culturally relevant television show.

"Driving to auditions that are anywhere from six to eight hours away, maybe even sometimes twice a week. So, you're living in Atlanta, but you're driving to New Orleans for auditions. I'm talking one-liners. When you talk about the grind. When you talk about work ethic. When you talk about being committed. That's where you learn because you are grateful."

—*Melissa Ponzio, Actor,* Teen Wolf, Chicago Fire

When I reflect upon work ethic, I often think of a famous quote from Robert De Niro's directorial debut, *A Bronx Tale*. After his character's son asks him if he has talent, De Niro tells the kid he has all the talent in the world. This prompts the boy to ask if he can be a pro baseball player someday. De Niro responds, "The saddest thing in life is wasted talent." He adds that the rest is up to working hard and doing "the right thing." In an ironic and sad twist of life imitating art, the actor Lillo Brancato, who played the boy, a total natural who was capable of going toe-to-toe with legends like De Niro and Chazz Palminteri, got mixed up with drugs later in life. He and a friend got involved with a burglary that resulted in an off-duty police officer being shot and killed. He served eight years in prison, with his life as he knew it forever changed. Talent is not worth much if it isn't attached to work ethic and values.

Top Three Takeaways

1. If you love something, you will *want* to work hard at it and be the best you can be. Having passion for something makes the work not feel like work.

2. Fear is a great motivator. If you pretend danger doesn't exist, your fear will freeze you when you're faced with danger.

3. A massive volume of work and preparation can serve as an insurance policy against nerves, fear, and unforeseen hiccups that are certain to arise in the course of a challenge.

CHAPTER

3

Performance, Anxiety, and Instinct

"We make decisions based on fear and we make them based on hope. And when we look back on our lives, the choices we made based on fear never work out."

—*Eric Christian Olsen, Actor*

While it may seem natural for an actor to include a chapter about performance in his book, the bold fact is that performance, the accompanying anxiety that goes with it, and the instinct used in the choices we make pertain to *everyone*. It's natural to examine performance and instinct in relation to actors and athletes; nevertheless, they are likely affecting the quality of *your* life right now. Regardless of our profession, most of us are overtly rewarded or punished depending on our ability to perform when it counts. Everyone's quality of life is directly correlated to how well they perform.

There are two common denominators behind the ability to perform well in any circumstance: overcoming anxiety, and honing your instincts. When you're focused on serving, helping, listening to, or engaging with any*one* or any*thing* besides yourself, you have a shot at success. But if you turn your head, even for a split second, you can lose the thread and watch your performance crumble before your very eyes.

Two Sides of the Same Coin

At my high school back in the late 1980s, there was a massive chasm between athletes and those involved in the theater. The social groups were separated into "jocks" and "dramies." The reason John Hughes's movies, like *The Breakfast Club* and *Pretty in Pink*, struck a chord with audiences is that they reflected a societal truth. Students definitely uttered snarky comments like, "He's just a dumb jock" or, "Dramies are such freaks." What I've discovered over two decades as a professional actor, however, is that there are *huge* similarities between athletic performers and artistic performers. Both of them, in their best moments, have a certain lack of fear and a touch of something beyond the purely physical world. There is much to learn about anxiety, and how to manage it, from both of these camps.

Despite my awareness that I was not a naturally gifted athlete like many of my friends, I was pegged as one of the jocks in high school. I played sports throughout the year and I was proud of my work ethic and my dedication to my teams.

"And that's when it clicked with me. I thought, 'These are not super *heroes*. These are just men that can do super things.'"

—*Christopher J. Burns, MD, FACS,*
former US Navy SEAL

There is an aspect of elite performance that is otherworldly. Watching Michael Jordan play basketball, Lindsey Vonn ski, or thespians like Meryl Streep and Christian Bale knock a powerhouse role out of the park, it seems as though what they're doing is effortless. It *appears* so natural that many people believe they, too, could do it, if only given the opportunity. Many mistakenly believe that it didn't take much work to pull it off, but that's the magic of performance. The *work ethic* discussed in Chapter 2 is like the energy it takes to get a rocket off the ground and through the atmospheric barrier, but the *performance* is more like what happens once the rocket jettisons its big engine and enters the weightlessness of space.

The media, and many times the performers themselves, often downplay the amount of work required to create such graceful moments because work doesn't sell as well as glamour. Even the lifestyles of great performers give outsiders the image of them sipping cocktails on a beach when they're not busy dazzling the rest of us, but nothing could be further from the truth. The actors I know and respect are the exact opposite of the attention-seeking stereotype strolling down a red carpet. Many are introverted and most possess enormous intelligence. That intelligence may or may not lend itself to being book smart or great with numbers, but the acting greats have an understanding of the nuances of human behavior that is astounding. Which is why it's not shocking when so many actors who go back to school for their degrees after working professionally when they were young have diplomas from universities like Brown, Harvard, Yale, or Columbia.

I have discovered that a large percentage of the actors I've worked with over the years came from athletic backgrounds. Even many of those who did not play traditional team sports were once dancers or figure skaters, both of which require incredible athletic ability and physical discipline. I believe the commonality lies in the performance. The same elements that go into performing every Sunday on a football field, for example, exist every night in the theater. I've experienced pre-show jitters just before the curtain goes up in the same way I used to find myself nervous on a football sideline until I got in the game. Getting hit by an opponent knocked me out of my head and into my body the same way uttering my first line in a play grounded me to the stage in front of a large audience.

Similarities abound. The ways in which we combat our nerves in sports and the arts are shockingly similar. Physical and vocal warmups in the theater can be compared to calisthenics before an athletic contest. There is a reliance on your teammates and coaches in sports, and a reliance on your castmates and crew in any production. And yet in both arenas, ironically, the majority of accolades and excessive pay are given for individual performances. Players are judged for individual statistics such as points in basketball, home runs in baseball, or touchdowns in football. Likewise, actors are singled out for a particular performance. But in both cases, it is the team effort that is awarded the championship trophy or the Best Picture Oscar regardless of individual performances.

Perhaps the real root of why so many former athletes turn to acting once their sports careers end is their addiction to the spontaneity of live performance and the management of fear and nerves. Playing lacrosse beyond the high school level I learned that, while raw talent does matter, perhaps the most important contributor to success in sports is the mental game and one's ability to continue playing despite a physical setback or a bad bounce that costs one's team a game. I've found that to be true as an actor as well. While the ability to keep one's nerves in check in high-pressure auditions, or particularly high-stress days on set, is important, the ability to face the abyss of extended unemployment in a very fickle business without cracking is the real challenge. One of the biggest factors deciding the longevity of one's career is the mental game.

> "If you bomb, if you fail, it's okay. You just go back home, and you work again, and you go back. If it lands, if it kills ... you're just the happiest man on the planet."
> —*Gad Elmaleh, Stand-up Comedian, Actor,*
> *Voted Funniest Man in France*

Nowhere in acting is the thrill of the unknown more electric than live theater. As a young actor in New York City, much of my early work consisted of plays. Aside from a few legitimate off-Broadway runs, those plays were performed in black-box theaters or other spaces that were not exactly what one envisions when they imagine a life on the boards. Regardless of the venue, the electricity of live theater is ever-present. When I moved to Los Angeles in the fall of 2005 to continue my run on *The West Wing*, my career transitioned into consisting almost exclusively of film and TV work. But in the fall of 2007, Loretta Greco, who had directed me off-Broadway in New York, came to Los Angeles to audition actors for a production of David Mamet's *Speed-the-Plow*. It was to be performed that winter at the Geary Theater in San Francisco under the auspices of the American Conservatory Theater.

Not only have I had the opportunity to work on several Mamet plays in various classes over the years, but I had the good luck to be cast in that spring 2008 production of *Speed-the-Plow* at the Geary. Some of the houses I performed in while living in New York held less than 60 audience members. That intimacy carried its own brand of intimidation. But the Geary was a beast of a different nature to what I'd experienced before. Multiple tiers of balconies rise at a sharp vertical and the ornate decor harkens back to theaters of our past. It can seat an audience of more than a thousand. It is an incredible place to work, but its size and prestige definitely bring with them an added level of excitement or stress, depending on how you view them.

You Can Take the Kid Out of the Black Box ...

The fundamentals of preparing *Speed-the-Plow* were virtually the same as preparing for any other show. We began with a cast table read in front of the producers, then proceeded to break the show down into smaller parts before gradually building it back up to the complete show the audience would experience. The main difference between this and the smaller productions in which I had performed before was that our tech week was more extensive. This just meant that our "cue-to-cue" rehearsals, in which the cast moves to the spots on the stage where they'll be standing during lighting shifts and scenery changes for the technicians to calibrate and time their cues, took a little longer. Much like scaling a mom-and-pop business into a corporate enterprise, the bells and whistles may appear different, but the foundation upon which it is built is constructed in roughly the same manner.

The nature of Mamet's writing, and this play in particular, which we performed for 90 minutes straight with no intermission, is very demanding and detail oriented. My character only left the stage for a very brief time before re-entering for the climax, so it required a certain amount of stamina and energy as well. The heavy, metered dialogue, in which my co-star and I, our characters having had a long history together, finished each other's sentences, required massive amounts of rehearsal to get the timing right while giving the audience the illusion that we were ad-libbing. My castmate Andrew Polk, who is a regular on the Broadway circuit, and I would go to the gym and speed through the entire play multiple times a day, every day, while climbing side by side on StairMaster machines. Once the play was up on its feet, performing it was like being shot out of a cannon or getting on a speeding train for 90 minutes straight every night.

By the time we reached opening night, the performance had become a dance between our tiny cast (Polk, me, and Jessi Campbell) and each audience that packed the house. Rave reviews made us a hot ticket in town and every night felt like a new, slightly different high-wire act. The potential for disaster in live theater has an allure to both the audience and those performing for them. Much like professional sports that are being played in front of a stadium of tens of thousands of people and simultaneously broadcast to millions more, there is no guarantee that things won't fall apart at any given moment. At the same time, there is always present the possibility that we may witness greatness with our own eyes, as it unfolds.

While this danger is alluring, it can also be terrifying. I will admit that there were some nights where my thoughts would begin to spiral into what I have since heard meditation teachers describe as "monkey mind." Minutes before a show, I'd be bombarded by hysterical thoughts of potential disaster striking. For an actor, that disaster could translate to what actors call "going up" on one's lines, forgetting one's lines in front of a packed house. The thought of having nowhere to run and nowhere to hide can be nightmare-inducing. But, as my old acting teacher Terry Schreiber used to say, "Sometimes the roles we fear the most are the roles we *need* to take on." His logic was that all of the energy we use to hold ourselves back from a role we fear, once we commit, will propel us even further into that character. This theory applies to anything from the daring feats of a trapeze artist to a field goal kicker attempting to boot a ball through the uprights 60 yards away to win the Super Bowl. It also applies to going out on stage every night in front of a live audience.

The razor's edge of performance is perhaps best illustrated by a story Tony Robbins shares at his Unleash the Power Within seminar. He tells of his two similar, yet drastically different, conversations with Carly Simon and Bruce Springsteen. When he asked Simon about her paralyzing stagefright, she said, "I feel my heart start to palpitate, my palms get sweaty ... and I know a panic attack is coming on." When Robbins asked Springsteen about his famously long concerts and how he can get himself into peak state for a new crowd every night, Springsteen answered, "My heart starts to race, my palms get sweaty ... and I know I'm ready to take the stage." Two identical symptoms; two *opposite* associations and outcomes.

> "I trained eight hours a day seven days a week, two weeks off a year from the age of three until I officially retired at 16. And I had a hangup. I got really badly injured at 13 because I could not land a double axel ... I had this mental block ... and I would just ... that was all I would practice every day ... my parents sent me to sports psychologists and I had to listen to all these different tapes of visualization ... but I just could not do that one jump and it really became my biggest nightmare."
>
> —*Julie Benz, Actor,* Dexter
> *Former figure skater, ranked 13th*
> *at the 1988 US Championships*

A few of my own 10,000 "no"s have come from bouts with performance anxiety. To make the point that the *actual* stakes of a situation are not as important as the *perception* of danger in our own minds, I'll share one of my first performance hiccups from the third grade. It was not a proper production but merely my class performing some kind of staged reading of a very short play in front of other third graders. They were our audience. No parents were present. The older and younger grades at our school weren't even aware this was happening. And yet, I can still remember the nervous feeling I had in my body. At a certain point I was to say, "If at first you don't succeed, try, try again." I did so, and we moved on. Somehow, however, the same cue came back around to me a minute later and I found myself saying the line for the second time. We all smirked, as would be expected from kids, but we stuck with it ... until it came around again.

As the line came out of me for the third time in three minutes, I snorted and keeled over, laughing so uncontrollably that I was crying.

It may have been compounded by the fact that the line itself described exactly what we were doing. The entire audience of third graders watched as everyone in the "play" broke down in giddy laughter. We were stuck in a loop and we couldn't get out. Eventually, we made it through the piece and it didn't leave much of a scar on my psyche. It just serves as a reminder of the slippery slope of performing, regardless of age, time, place, or audience.

Doesn't Take Much to Be Knocked Off Course

Another anxiety hiccup took place on a night of one-act plays I did in the West Village with a group of friends. It was a relatively tiny production and the play I was performing was about two cater waiters. Romantically involved, they were questioning their relationship as they worked together on New Year's Eve of 1999, heading into the new millennium. I had only been dating my now-wife, who is not and has never been in my business, for a few months when I invited her to bring her parents to see me perform. Most likely distracted by the thought that they were present in the theater, at one point my scene partner said her line and I went completely blank. I had no idea what came next. It felt like an eternity, a nightmare. Though it was probably just a second or two, in those seconds, I had thoughts of my new relationship ending because no parent would want their daughter dating, much less marrying, a guy who says he's an actor but can't even remember his lines. Somehow, I slowed my brain down enough to recall the circumstances of the play and this moment. Magically, my brain fed the line to me and I promptly spit it out. The show must go on, and it did.

After the curtain, everyone gathered in the lobby and talked about the play as is typical. When I asked my now-in-laws if they were nervous when I forgot my line, they stared at me with puzzled expressions on their faces. They had no idea what I was talking about. What felt like an abysmal gaffe to me went completely unnoticed by the audience.

There Are Hit Shows ... and There Are Hits in Shows

The run of *Speed-the-Plow* was a hit and every night different VIPs would show up as well as friends and family, sometimes even those from the East Coast, who flew in to see the show. One night after the show, I learned that one of my older brother's friends had been in the audience. When I asked him what he thought, he said, "It was great." There was a slight pause, and then he continued, "I mean, that punch is a mile away from you, but other than that it was great." He was referring to a staged fight in which my character gets punched and knocked down. Once he's on the ground, he gets kicked in the ribs. I had a packet of fake blood, which I bit so that when I came up holding my nose, the blood would run down from my nostrils as though I had a bleeder. I allowed this comment to pull my focus from the task at hand, which would have a drastic effect on the following afternoon's Sunday matinee and prove just how dangerous it can be to try to please an audience.

> "Last night you asked for a cup of coffee with that line. Tonight you asked for a laugh."
> —*Uta Hagen, Legendary Theater Director and Acting Teacher, explaining why an actor failed to get laughs on a joke that landed the previous night*

In that performance, when the punch came, I thrust myself back with a violent jerk and hit the deck in an effort to prove my brother's friend wrong. Whereas I normally landed close to the foot of the stage, this time I felt my momentum carrying me further. As I was rolling over I saw the ceiling of the Geary passing by, far above me. Then I felt my body leave the stage, the ceiling still spinning. Looking down as I jettisoned through the air, I was simultaneously debating whether an actor could fall off a stage while contemplating the possibility that I was going to land in the lap of the old man sitting in the front row, when … *crack*! My nose smashed into the man's knee. You can't make this stuff up.

I was sure I had broken my nose. There was a collective gasp from the audience, then a pause. Knowing the show must go on, I hopped back up onto the stage, causing another gasp to ripple though the theater. I took my usual fetal position and, on cue, Polk began to "kick" me in the ribs the way he always did. I bit the blood packet and, when I came up, fake blood pouring down my face, I thought one of the elderly matinee audience members was going to faint. A follow-up X-ray revealed that my nose did not, in fact, break. But those people paid for live theater, and dammit, that's what we gave 'em!

Instincts: Trust Your Gut

The best performances usually occur when supposed accidents happen and people are forced to think and act on the spot. Instinct is a performer's best tool. A mishap allows an audience to witness another human work themselves out of a jam in live time, which is what happened in that particular performance of *Speed-the-Plow*. This happens on stages and sets as well as sports fields. In high school, playing lacrosse against the defending Connecticut State Champions on their home turf, our game went into overtime. When the best player on our team took a shot, the opposing team's goalie blocked it and the deflected ball seemed to hang in the air in slow motion. Without thought, I reached up with my stick, got ahold of it, and shot it into the opponent's goal. Before I knew it, I was tackled by my teammates and buried on the bottom of a pile. My shot had just won the game. But here's what I remember: while I didn't play horribly, it wasn't my best game ever. In fact, I mistakenly thought the overtime period was five minutes so I didn't realize that we were in sudden death. When my teammates tackled me and piled on in celebration I was just as surprised as the other team's shocked parents. The result may have been monumental, but my "performance" was merely that of a player reacting to a loose ball.

I have observed repeatedly, while watching my son's youth baseball games over the years, that kids who typically don't see themselves as good athletes or baseball players make their best plays when the ball is smashed directly in their direction. With no time for their brains to react, their bodily instincts kick in and, seemingly magically, they come up with a huge play that shocks all of the parents in the stands.

While some people are more naturally instinctive than others, I believe that if one can see the value in using their instinct, they can seek out other likeminded individuals who will help them cultivate it even more. When I interviewed Chip Taylor, the man who wrote the hit songs "Wild Thing" and "Angel of the Morning" on his way to the Songwriter's Hall of Fame as well as putting out an astounding 29 albums over a five-decade span, I mistakenly described what he does as writing poetry and matching it to music. He corrected me and described it like this:

> "I would pick up the guitar, or in some manner hum some nonsense things to myself and wait until some words fell in together with some melody. And sometimes it made no sense at all, but if it gave me a chill, then I would continue with it."
>
> —*Chip Taylor*

Tony Blauer, the self-defense expert I mentioned in Chapter 2, shared a story with me on *10,000 NOs* that described this very phenomenon. He was teaching Special Ops Military Forces tactical moves in removing the threat of a loaded weapon at close range in combat. When one of the operators continued to take slightly longer than everyone else to disarm the gun, Blauer was perplexed. While a split second may not sound like a long time, in this case it was the difference between life and death. When Blauer honed in on what this operator was doing, the man became defensive. After observing him repeatedly, Blauer realized this soldier was taking extra steps that were adding the unwanted time to the maneuver. It was only then, after Blauer pressed the issue, that the operator revealed that he had been a former Judo World Champion. It turned out that he was unaware of the extra steps he was taking because they had become instinctive after years of extensive training. Instinct is learnable.

Perhaps the most famous example of instinct in film history centers on Marlon Brando while shooting a scene with Eva Marie Saint in the classic 1954 film *On the Waterfront*. Brando plays a tough ex-boxer who is now barely making ends meet by finding sparse work at the docks as a longshoreman. In one scene, he and Saint are walking through a park in Hoboken, New Jersey, as a romance is budding between their characters. In the middle of one take, Saint accidentally dropped her white glove to the ground. Rather than call "cut," director Elia Kazan let the scene play out. Without breaking stride, Brando squatted down, picked up the dainty white glove and, as they continued to talk, attempted to stretch the glove over his own big meat hook. As the scene continues, this simple gesture of his big hand not fitting into her dainty glove says more about their entire tragic love story than could have been accomplished with ten pages of dialogue. Brando's swift and instinctive gesture shows us that these two won't survive together because they're from different sides of the track. It's held up as one of the greatest scenes in cinematic history.

Brando adapted in the moment. He didn't stop or complain that it wasn't a perfect take. He incorporated the "mistake," and in doing so, his willingness to allow the chaos of real life to enter the scene made it more authentic than they ever could have planned ahead of time. Filmmakers and actors call this a "happy accident," and the greats actually look for these opportunities. Lesser artists might have called "cut," choosing to remain in the safety of their preplanned ideas. Legends like Kazan, Brando, and Saint knew the value of instinct and that's how they gave us movie magic.

While some people look at top performers who have repeatedly produced incredible results under pressure as being different from the average person, these superstars are not exempt from feeling nervous. Every time they take the field or the stage, they are taking the same risk as you and I: they are putting themselves in a position where failure *is* an option. The quality that they have cultivated better than most, however, is the ability to focus and remain relaxed while under said pressure and to rely on their instincts. It is no easy task, and sometimes even incredible training cannot solve the problem of performance anxiety. It is a psychological battle in which fear never helps you unless it is transformed into positive energy that welcomes risk rather than hiding from it.

Top Three Takeaways

1. Performance is about the relationship between the performer, their thoughts, and the audience or crowd. Regardless of a venue's size, there is always potential for performance meltdowns to occur.

2. Even superstar performers experience the terrifying fear of bombing or failing to execute. We must all learn to manage our fears and channel that energy to benefit the performance.

3. Training and preparation are necessary components to performance, but once the performance is in progress it is all about being in the moment and trusting your instincts.

CHAPTER

4

Discipline and Training

"Until you're crystal clear on what you're willing to give up for your goals, you'll never achieve them."

—Craig Ballantyne, Author/Speaker
The Perfect Day Formula

W hile it must be admitted that training, even if it is intense and focused, will not always bring home a gold medal or create an Oscar-worthy performance, it is a necessary component to excel in any field. It can come in many different forms, depending on your goals and style, but training instills discipline, and discipline breeds consistency.

The Game Is Won or Lost Before You Even Take the Field

The mental game I've leaned upon as an actor was honed over years and years as an athlete. Putting up with, and playing through, hardships and physical pain is necessary if you want to be a contender by the time playoffs roll around. Showing up twice a day to football practice in the middle of August when the blistering sun was beating down, knowing classmates were at the beach, my teammates and I developed grit. Our job as athletes, which is the same for me as an actor or for *anyone* attempting to attain *any* goal, was to tap into our passion on a regular basis by remaining focused on our long-term goal. This is how we got ourselves through the temporary pain. Late into a football season, or early in a lacrosse season, when the East Coast weather was cold and wet, we found ways to continue trudging through because that was what was necessary to perform well on game days and remain standing at the end of our season.

The best actors I know do not just rehearse when inspiration strikes. The best have a discipline that is enviable. Most have specific regimens or a particular approach to their work, but these can be as varied and unique as the actors themselves. The quality that *all* of them possess is a constant quest to be better than they were yesterday and to learn from those who are better than them. Since the advent of the smartphone, my close friend Chris Messina, who is one of the most disciplined and talented actors I know, has sent me a steady stream of texts with links to articles about and interviews with legendary actors we love. When a new actor arrives upon the scene with a great performance, I am sure to hear about it from Messina because he is eternally obsessed with mastering the craft of acting. These texts serve as a daily reminder to me that there is always someone out there from whom I can learn. They push me to know that, somewhere, someone is working harder than me or just possesses more talent. If I lose my discipline, I lose my edge. And if that happens, it is less likely that I will be able to put food on the table on a consistent basis.

"A great fallacy regarding progress is that it is defined
by constant forward motion in the same direction."
—*Alison Levine*, New York Times *Bestselling Author,*
On the Edge: Leadership Lessons from
Everest and Other Extreme Environments

While there is a competitive spirit linked to chasing something, other people's successes should not deem our accomplishments to be null and void. Instead, the competition is internal,
which is why the elite are competing against the best version
of themselves. Whether it's Michael Jordan, Meryl Streep, or
Christian Bale, underneath the pursuit lies passion. It is a fer-
vent quest to find something that flows in a way that cannot be
grabbed or handled. And, while the best come closest, they are
the first to agree that there is no such thing as perfection and our
work is never done. The manifestation of this internally competitive pursuit comes in the form of training and discipline.

Buy Speed

Every high achiever I've sat down with, regardless of their profession, agrees that rather than try to reinvent the wheel, it is wiser
to stand on the shoulders of giants in the pursuit of excellence.
This is usually done by finding coaches, teachers, and mentors
who have been where you want to go or helped others achieve
their goals. While the best version of this is a flesh-and-blood
mentor, you can also easily find books and interviews from legends you admire. In this day and age, where virtually anything can
be found on the Internet, our heroes, role models, and mentors
are only a click away. With the advent of social media, not only
can you *study* the giants in your field or find tape of them doing
what they do, you can many times interact with them as they
have become increasingly accessible through blogs, live posts,

mastermind groups, and weekend retreats. The excuse that you have no access no longer holds up.

There is an epidemic, however, that impedes the growth of many people. Ironically, it is perhaps even more prevalent today than in the past, despite the fact that everything is accessible. This epidemic results from the lack of understanding that there is a difference between something being *in*formational versus *trans*formational. Informational means that you can read all the books, listen to all the podcasts, and go to all the seminars you can afford and still walk away unchanged. Transformational means you are *implementing* the principles you're learning about and *applying* them to your life. This is why mentors are so valuable. Because they can give you hands-on accountability and allow you to "buy speed," as *10,000 NOs* podcast guest Sharran Srivatsaa describes it.

Srivatsaa knows about buying speed because, with the help of mentors, he took Teles Properties, *Inc.* magazine's fastest growing real estate brokerage in California, from $350 million in annual revenue to $3.5 billion in revenue in just five years. Not only did Srivatsaa learn speed-hacks from CEOs he sought out and paid for access to their knowledge, but he implemented everything he learned by instilling an incredible, company-wide culture of discipline. With monthly, weekly, and daily practices, Srivatsaa was able to teach the speed he had bought and increase his company's value ten times in a time frame that previously seemed impossible.

Talking the talk as if you are an expert is easy. Listening to an expert, like Srivatsaa, is inspiring. It is also easy, because it doesn't cost you anything. Actually applying these lessons to your own life is the biggest challenge because it requires discipline. Discipline implies that there is a cost to attaining things that are sought after by many. It may cost you time, money, freedom, or any combination of all of these plus more, but it will cost you. Discipline carries with it a sacrifice because in order to do one thing, you may need to cut out many other things. A lack of discipline, along with self-limiting beliefs that I was unaware I'd been carrying around with me, is why I have failed many times in my life. But rather than lacerate myself for my failures, I will share this one story of a success I earned through discipline.

If You're Gonna Talk the Talk,
Ya Gotta Walk the Walk

After a long drought of unemployment, I found myself in the enviable position of winning the role of Jason Alan Ross on the Netflix comedy series *Huge in France*. What I loved about this role was the change my character had to go through from the beginning of the season to the end. When he first appears on screen, Jason might erroneously be pegged as an alpha male bully who knows his way around a gym but has no awareness of his own vulnerability. But by episode two, his tough and confident exterior begins to peel away with such speed that we soon realize this is a man whose entire persona is built upon a house of cards. He is anything but secure.

After reading the entire eight-episode season, I knew there was only one way to fully pull off this portrayal. It would require incredible discipline to get it done, but given the fact that Jason's identity was so tied up with his external appearance, I knew that my performance would suffer if I didn't get myself significantly more fit than I was at the time I was cast. While my own workout and diet regimen is relatively consistent, to play Jason I needed to be on a different level. With his acting career in the pits, Jason has been relegated to being a glorified babysitter to his girlfriend's son. His primary task is to mentor this spoiled teenager through a modeling career mostly by keeping his gym routine and very specific food intake on track. In exchange for his efforts, he receives a small stipend and the privilege to keep living in his girlfriend's mansion. His lot in life is pretty pathetic and the way I saw it, his physique was one of the only things he had going for himself. Not only did I have a target body composition, but also a specific date by which I needed to hit it. The day I was cast, I was given a shooting schedule, which included two comical—mostly naked—sex scenes I had to shoot in just 22 days.

> "I can't let Jason Alan Ross raise my son. He worships
> this Jason guy. He waxes, he tans. How can I compete?"
>
> *Gad*, Huge in France

While the waxing of my chest, stomach, and arms was almost as painful as it was funny, the *real* work lay in the adherence to a training and eating regimen. My friend and top strength coach Jay Ferruggia assigned me to a six-day-a-week training program, but that was not much different from my normal routine. Contrary to what most friends and acquaintances thought when they saw me begin to transform, the real challenge was not in the gym but the eating regimen. Ferruggia is one of the most deliberate and specific people I know, which is how he maintains his incredible physique year-round in his mid-forties. It was no surprise, therefore, when he tweaked my weight training and dialed in on my diet to the point where I knew what I'd be eating every day for every meal for the next 22 days. Just because I expected it, did not make it any easier to execute.

It took a lot of discipline for me not to abandon Ferruggia's program when friends, seeing me shed weight, began to say I was getting "too skinny." If they had known my history of not being able to pack on the pounds and gain muscle in high school sports, they would have realized that I *hate* the word "skinny" when it's used to describe me. The mere mention of even a temporary weight loss for me is probably what has thwarted any previous attempts like this one from succeeding. Ironically, Jay's plan wasn't starving me at all. I was eating four meals a day, but the timing, the food combinations, the water intake, and the training style were producing different results. One of the biggest lessons I learned through this experience was that a large amount of preparation and planning mitigates the reliance on willpower. Preparing my meals in bulk ahead of time so they would be ready and waiting for me at the right times made it automatic. My whiny brain was not given the chance to chime in and clamor for more, or different, food. Because I trusted Ferruggia and our collective vision of where I needed to be by day 22, I maintained my discipline. Having the target so clear in my mind was instrumental to keeping me focused despite the attempts of my inner critic to sabotage me.

The little hacks and details that make an endeavor less challenging are funny and surprising. Had I been able to afford a private chef, this might have been a lot easier, but that was not the case. Instead, I purchased slightly higher-end Tupperware containers that inspired me more than the cheaper ones we typically used in our house. While this may sound nonsensical, the additional pride I was taking in my food prep, even down to the containers that were being used to hold it, helped me to be even more invested in my mission. I would also purchase chicken breast in bulk and, much to my wife's amusement and annoyance, fill the entire grill with it to prep for several days' worth of meals. I would steam large amounts of spinach and cook large pots of white jasmine rice, the only carb I was allowed, so that I wouldn't waste time individually preparing each meal. The operation was astounding and eye-opening and reminded me why I didn't take the time to do this year-round.

The results, though, were more than physical. I texted Ferruggia shirtless selfies every few days so he could chart my progress and tweak the program if need be (he was on the road, as he often is, so this is how he kept track of my progress). While we were both serious about this joint mission, we had some laughs over the selfies, mostly at my expense. The beauty was that the changes were not only occurring on the surface. I discovered that the *actions* I was taking taught me more about my character than any amount of reading I could have done as research. Because I was actually doing what Jason would do, I began to have firsthand experiences that gave me insight into Jason's self-involved psyche. I would later shoot scenes where Jason is drinking protein shakes and chattering incessantly about his diet that sounded frighteningly similar to the interactions I was now having with my wife as a result of this obsessive regimen.

> "Viv: See? This is why you can't handle acting. You go too far with it.
> Jason: There is no such thing as going too far!!!"
>
> Huge in France, *Netflix*
> *Season 1: Ep. 4, Episode Quatre*

One such interaction came near the Fourth of July, as we were getting ready to go to our friends' house for a day of swimming and barbecuing. Unbeknownst to my wife, I had snuck my prepackaged chicken breast and spinach-filled container into the bottom of our beach bag. Finding it, she looked at me, incredulous. "You're not seriously taking your own food to their house, are you?" I replied, "What?! This is what I need to do!" Anyone who has seen the series will remember many such scenes where Jason, a self-proclaimed method actor, is vehemently defending his self-involved actions to his girlfriend, Viv, claiming that they are a necessary ingredient for his art. Through discipline and training, I had found my character's voice and mannerisms. As one friend jokingly ribbed me after seeing a scene like the one above, "Cuts pretty close to the bone, huh?"

While I hope this story is funny and entertaining for you, there are many lessons within it about the power of discipline and training, and how that power can many times exceed our expectations. I have a brother, as well as many friends from college and adult life, who are in the finance industry. Jokes are often made about how different he is from my sister and me despite the fact that we are blood-related. The general thrust of the jokes is that he is extremely detail-oriented and uber-disciplined, whereas I can be more "go with the flow." While there are pluses and minuses to being either more structured or looser, I believe there is a need for both. I'd venture to say that all three of us have different combinations of both sides. But while people perceive artists to be "touchy feely" I have found that the greats, while incredibly sensitive and open to spontaneity, are also incredibly disciplined and attentive to details. Training is the concrete process in which those details are adhered to and systemized.

The Right Way Is the Way that Works for You

Ferruggia created a system that worked for me by keeping it simple. Before designing my training and diet regimens, he first asked me to define my goal. When my muddled answer, that I wanted to gain muscle *and* be more defined, contradicted itself, he didn't placate me. Given my tight timeline, he forced me to *make a choice*. His advice was to get more lean because it would be more effective on camera for what I needed. He took the guess-work out and made the plan easy for me to follow. Even though he has worked with others in more intricate and sophisticated ways, he knew I didn't have the time or bandwidth to do that. Instead, he laid it out for me in a basic way so I could follow it to the letter. He knew that discipline was the most important factor, so he designed it so a monkey could follow it. It was so pragmatic that there was nothing to argue with. Either do it, or don't do it. The choice was mine.

> "The first time you walk into a gym you don't say, 'Because I can't squat 225 or 315 *now* it means I'll never do it.' Same thing with this. Anybody can get better at this stuff. You track your squats or chin-ups at the gym, so I would say, 'Okay, how many compliments did I give?' And I'd write it in my journal. 'How many times did I start a conversation with somebody, in the line at Starbucks or at the grocery store?' I'd just push myself every day. And, now, that's my thing. It's super easy now. It was just work, that's all it was. Just repetition."
>
> —*Jay Ferruggia, Strength Coach and Speaker,*
> *on being a former introvert turned superconnector*

When I was in the third grade, my teacher gave my class an assignment in the beginning of the school year, due at the end of each semester. Not being much of a disciplinarian, she never really mentioned it after that. If she did, I certainly didn't hear her. The assignment involved reading short stories in our textbooks throughout the semester and answering six to eight questions per story. It was the kind of assignment that would have been easy if it were done throughout the year, but by the end of the semester, when we were reminded of the due date, I was caught completely off-guard. Not ones to mess around when it came to my education, my parents did not give in to my pleas to finish it after going to a popular annual carnival in our town.

Instead, they set up a folding table in my bedroom and essentially locked me inside until all my work was done.

After much twisting, turning, and schmoozing to try get out of it, I realized I had no choice. Once I settled down, I actually found a joy, and even comfort, in the work. I liked the feeling of progress. When I finished, I felt a real sense of pride and accomplishment. I told my parents I wished I had read the stories earlier because they were actually good. I was not lying to them; the discipline really did feel great. And yet, at the end of the next semester, unbelievably, I had done it again. As the due date approached, I hadn't touched the stories. And, again, my parents locked me up and threw away the key until I came out with all the work complete.

Sometimes, because we are imperfect beings, we have to be taught lessons a lot more than once before we learn them. The universe has a way of continuing to throw the same lesson our way until we finally wise up and can handle it and move forward. If I hadn't learned my lesson by the end of the third grade, my fourth grade teacher, Ms. Taylor, whom everyone feared, was sent by the universe to do the trick. My Dad still reminds me that it is Ms. Taylor who changed the course of my life through sheer discipline. I got straight E's (for Excellent) and straight 1's (for good behavior) all year long. In fact, I excelled in school in general from then on. When my parents went to see Ms. Taylor for their parent-teacher conference that year, my Dad gestured to her head and asked, "Where are they?" Ms. Taylor looked confused until my father grinned and said, "Your horns." They all laughed and my parents thanked her profusely for having the tough love to teach me one of the most teachable difference-makers one can learn: the power of discipline and good study habits.

Discipline is necessary if not easy. While some have it naturally, it can be honed. Like nearly everything else in this book, it is simply a choice. When you get to the point that the actions you've been taking are no longer bringing you satisfaction or joy, you will likely be at the juncture where you decide to give discipline a try. Once you begin, you may never stop because you'll learn that structure will bring you freedom, and every habit that you choose to give up will be replaced by a better habit that brings you joy rather than misery and frustration.

Top Three Takeaways

1. Discipline requires clarity and demands that you make choices. You can't have your cake and eat it, too.
2. Planning and preparation reduce the need to exercise your willpower.
3. Remaining laser-focused on a goal through the finish line will reap you more rewards than you realize when you initially set out to run the race.

CHAPTER
5

Risk

"If you want to take the island, you need to burn the boats."

—*Tony Robbins*, Unleash the Power Within

In 2016, my wife and I were invited to Tony Robbins's Unleash the Power Within seminar in San Jose, California. There was much excitement throughout the weekend as we got to know, and fire-walk with, some impressive people sitting in our section. Actor Gerard Butler, World Champion Triathlete Siri Lindley, and physical therapist and strength coach Rory Cordial, who is so good at his job that Beyoncé and Jay-Z bring him with them on their world tours to keep them limber and healthy, were among the folks with whom we were fortunate enough to connect. I was inspired enough to jumpstart my then-nascent idea for the *10,000 NOs* podcast, and many of those people have since been guests on the show. That weekend, the majority of topics that were covered resonated for me, but the one that really stood out was the idea behind burning the boats.

Conquer or Die

It was so appropriate for me at that time because we had just left our rent-stabilized apartment on the beach of Santa Monica earlier that week to move into a house in the neighborhood where our kids had been commuting to school. While this move doubled our monthly expenses, we knew the risk we were taking was an attempt to put our kids and our family in a neighborhood where we could thrive the most.

The idea behind "burning the boats" is simple: conquer or die. The literal burning of the boats refers to a historical invasion, although there are disputes as to which one. One possibility is Spanish conqueror Hernán Cortés's conquest of the Aztec Empire in 1519. With the intent to seize treasure, Cortés led a large expedition to invade what we now know as Mexico. His invaders were outnumbered by the warriors defending the shores. Cortés ordered his men to burn their ships before taking the island. Within two years, the Aztec Empire belonged to Spain. For me, the lesson is that there is no opportunity for the glory of victory if one does not place him or herself in a position where he or she may face real danger or defeat.

I see the core principle behind "burning the boats" applying to *any* decision, large or small, that we may face throughout the course of one day, or our entire life. In the early 2000s, while struggling with the decision of whether I should remain in New York City or move to Los Angeles, a trusted confidant simply looked at me and said, "If you move to Los Angeles, you'll miss out on opportunities here in New York ... And if you remain here in New York, you'll miss out on opportunities in Los Angeles." It was comically simple, yet true. No matter how much money I pay an acting coach or therapist, or how much advice I seek from a colleague or mentor, ultimately the decisions I make come down to *me* and *my* desires, no one else's. And every single one of those decisions contains risk, whether I'm aware of it or not.

The challenge is not in *understanding* this simple principle. The challenge is that most people would rather remain comfortable than risk financial failure or physical and psychological pain. The truth is that we all need to take risks. But *how much* risk should you take? And *when* you should take it? There is no guaranteed correct answer, but it's just as important to keep in mind that while passion and courage are essential, so are intelligence, wisdom, patience, and strategy. If you veer too far to either side of this spectrum, you can end up flaming out before you've reached your goal or never stretching enough to have great opportunities.

If ever there were a guest on the *10,000 NOs* podcast whom I would deem a risk-taker, it's Alison Levine. Not only was she the captain of the first US female expedition to climb Mount Everest, but she has completed the adventure grand slam, which entails climbing the highest peak on every continent, and lived to write about it (in her *New York Times* Best-Selling book, *On the Edge: Leadership Lessons from Mount Everest*). What makes her story even more remarkable is that she was found to have a hole in her heart as a youngster. While her entire life and career revolves around risk, she still preaches safety and sensibility while simultaneously pushing the boundaries of her capabilities.

> "Your plan is outdated as soon as it's finished. So it is
> good to plan 'cause that can help you get on track or
> stay on track, but you cannot be hell-bent on sticking

to that plan no matter what. You have to adjust, change
your direction or take action based on the situation at
the time."

—Alison Levine, Mountain Climber, Speaker, Author

After the rollercoaster of 2001, when I proposed to my
now-wife in late August only to face the loss of friends and peace
in New York City on September 11, I was cast on *The Sopranos*
just before the start of 2002. Getting that call on December 20,
2001, was, and will probably remain, the most dramatic "yes"
I have ever had in the business. This is not only due to it coming
on the heels of the biggest tragedy our country has ever faced or
The Sopranos' place in cultural history at the time, but also to my
relative youth. Despite being thirty years old, I still possessed a
naive perspective on my career, fame, and life in general. While
I continue to get excited about jobs to this day, the excitement
pales in comparison to milestones like watching the births of my
children and other significant familial experiences. Also, at this
point I have peeked far enough behind the curtain of Hollywood
to realize that the effects of big wins, while always welcome, are
much less dramatic and life-altering than I imagined they would
be when I was younger. The result of landing *The Sopranos* was
that, having weathered the depressing events of 2001, 2002 felt
like a new beginning for me. After seven years slugging it out
in New York City, I was finally able to tell strangers that I was
an actor without having to include my usual ten-minute mono-
logue that explained where I bartended, where I waited tables,
and where I took scene-study classes. It felt like the struggle
was over.

The struggle, it turns out, was *not* over. And yet, this break
was big and it did help me considerably. But my story of getting
The Sopranos is about the risks that were taken to put me in that
audition room in the first place.

After four years of college that had prepared me for some high-paying jobs in professions I had little interest in, choosing to be an actor without giving myself a Plan B is probably the first risk I took. Not long after moving to New York, I scored a big break when a film in which I was cast as the lead turned from non-union to SAG (Screen Actors Guild) because actor Frank Vincent (*Raging Bull*, *Goodfellas*, *Casino*) signed on. Up until this time, none of the projects I had found in *Backstage* magazine paid me or did anything to raise my profile. But this film turned out to be different. While it didn't earn me a penny, *The North End* had a festival run that helped move me out of total obscurity and into a smaller pool of actors. In post-production, when the filmmakers told me they were short on cash, I risked my reputation by going to my brother and his friends, who owned and operated the successful midtown bar that I'd been tending, asking for the money that was needed to finish the film.

They stepped up and we contributed almost $20,000 combined, including $2,000 from my own hard-earned stash. I did not have a lot of money at this time. I was living in a fifth-floor walk-up, rent-stabilized apartment on the Upper East side of Manhattan and supporting myself by bartending and working the counter at California Pizza Kitchen.

Raising this money solidified my relationship with the filmmakers, who then tapped me to play the lead in their follow-up film, which would be shooting in Italy. I paid for myself to take a bus up to Boston for multiple table reads of the Italy film before production would move to Italy to begin shooting.

Don't Take It Personally, Take It Professionally

As that second film got closer to production, the filmmakers hired casting director Georgianne Walken to help them find their cast. She was not aware of my work at the time, but when the filmmaker brothers told her that I was their choice to play the lead, she talked them out of it. Instead, she convinced them to hire an actor she believed was more suited to the role. The film was made in Italy without me, and Walken was not my favorite person. She was also, however, the casting director for *The Sopranos*, and in the years that followed she brought me in to audition for various small parts on the show. While I was never cast, I was usually called back to read for the producers.

In 2001, when the audition came in for Cousin Brian, a much bigger part than the previous roles I'd auditioned for on the show, I read the material and thought, "I could play this guy." The audition material consisted of mostly financial jargon as my character was a financial advisor. He was tasked with pitching his cousin's husband, who happened to be Tony Soprano, ways in which he could invest his money. Many of my friends from college worked on Wall Street and the majority of the customers I'd been slinging drinks for at the bar spent their days on the stock exchange. This gave me the confidence that I could handle the lingo and lend credence to this role. I then took my next risk: rather than bartend the night before my initial audition, I gave my shift away. While this may not sound like a big sacrifice, at the time that was worth three to four hundred dollars that I could have put toward my rent and other expenses.

Given the fact that, statistically speaking, I could go in for 30 to 50 auditions without landing a job, choosing to give that money up for a *chance* at scoring this role—I wanted to be as fresh as possible—might be viewed as a dumb risk. However you view it, that risk ended up paying off when that initial audition impressed Walken enough that I was sent to the producers with her championing me to get the role. (More on that later, but I got the gig. Eventually.) And 2002 *did* end up being a monumental year: I shot the majority of my work on *The Sopranos*, did my first legitimate off-Broadway play, and got married only eight days before all of my episodes began to air on HBO. It was a very high peak amid a career full of valleys, and it led to what I *thought* was going to turn into a triumphant mountaintop in 2003.

What Goes Up Must Come Down

If my 2003 could be placed on a line graph, it would look like the backside of a mountain, a high point followed by a sharp drop-off. My confidence and momentum remained sky-high through March and then, by April, plummeted to a low that rivaled that of early 2001. Due to the run of the off-Broadway play in 2002, which began rehearsing just before our wedding, my wife and I postponed our honeymoon to Hawaii until January 2003. So, despite that small sacrifice, we began the new year in luxury, counting the blessings of the previous year, excited about the big risk we were about to take—relocating to Los Angeles so I could be there for my first pilot season. That proved to be a *huge* swing and a miss.

The combination of having just gotten married and my wife not being passionate about her career in ad sales prompted me to convince her to quit her job and come with me to Los Angeles for a few months. I was riding high off of *The Sopranos*, having received a lot of attention for it on the streets of New York. My agents and I believed that it was time to "strike while the iron was hot." So, after our honeymoon, we illegally sublet our rental apartment in New York and took on a sublease from one of my high school friends who was looking to unload her place in LA. It was not exactly glamorous, but the palm trees made up for it and, most importantly, I wanted to be right in the mix as they began to cast all of the following season's series now that my career seemed to be on track.

Pilot season 2003 began with a frenzy. Never before had I received so much attention or had as many shots at potential gigs. Everywhere I went I felt like a celebrity. I remember driving to Burbank for a meeting with all the SVPs of casting at NBC and having them gush over me to the point where one of them said, "Oh my God, Cousin Brian! You *have* to sign a headshot for the guy who cuts our promo videos! He *loves* you!" I figured I was going to have to fight potential employers off with a stick due to all the demand on me. After all, they *loved* me … right? February flew by, March continued the frenzy but it slowly began to grind to a halt so that by April, not only did I *not* have a job, I had not tested for any pilots. In layman's terms, not testing means I never really came too close. The nearest I came to landing an actual job was when I was called back for what's known as a "mix-and-match session" for a "highly anticipated series." Even though I was never a part of it, that series, much like my pilot season, ended up being a bust anyway.

By the middle of April, we had rifled through more wedding money than I would like to admit, despite being frugal. While I desperately hoped for more opportunities, I was painfully aware that this risk was not going to work out the way I had imagined it. And while there is no silver lining at the end of this particular segment of my life, and I was destined to return to New York City with my tail between my legs, there is at least a small but worthy story about risk that I can share with you.

Free-fallin'

Knowing that pilot season was essentially over, we went down to Coronado to visit my college friend who was a Navy SEAL and stationed there. After spending the weekend with a large group that consisted of my buddy and his elite friends, one of them invited my wife and me to a Dodgers game the following Tuesday in LA, where he'd be parachuting into Dodger Stadium before the game.

> "You have to bet on yourself because if you don't believe enough in yourself, nobody else will. We're all gonna die. The question is: Are we all gonna live? I didn't want to look up from a hospital bed and wonder, why was I too scared to try?"
>
> —*Roger Fishman, Adventure Photographer,*
> *former Chief of Global Marketing, CAA*

Gus Kaminski was a Captain of the Navy SEAL Leapfrogs, their skydiving team. And after watching him and his teammates float onto the field at Dodger Stadium, my wife and I sat with him to watch the game. After telling him how envious I was that he could basically experience flight with a parachute, I lamented about how dead my schedule had become as we stuck around for one last chance at a show. Seeing an opening, he invited us back down to the San Diego area to skydive with him the next day. I wouldn't say that skydiving was necessarily on my bucket list, but when you have a personal connection to a Navy SEAL who is willing to show you and your new bride the ropes, you kind of have to take him up on it. After complaining of being bored by a lack of opportunities and excitement, we decided to take the plunge, literally.

Jumping out of a plane at 13,000 feet is a good way to die if you don't know what you're doing. But if you strap yourself to the Captain of the Leapfrogs, the chances of death diminish considerably. We were able to experience the thrill of flight without the usual risk that attends such a feat. It's not that we didn't take a risk—every skydive is a risk regardless of skill and experience—but we mitigated the chances of failure by seeking counsel and guidance from an expert who could lead the way. But having Kaminski did not remove the fear and excitement that occurs when the door is raised and the entire side of the plane is open to Earth far below. Nor did being strapped to him take away the extreme rush of rocking back and forth three times before launching myself into a backflip, then leveling out and free-falling for over a minute. For a leap to be considered a leap, it must contain the possibility of flight as well as the possibility of plummeting to the earth.

"Sacrifice hurts to the bone."
—*Dr. Christopher J. Burns, MD, FACS,*
Trauma Surgeon, former US Navy SEAL

Plummeting to the earth is something that I faced in a different way upon returning to New York City at the end of April 2003. The daydreams I'd had of my *Sopranos* stint leading to me sitting on Letterman's couch to discuss my latest blockbuster film came crashing down into the reality of unemployment. The Buzz of my success was gone. The only thing left was the decision to remove my ego and find a way to start putting food on the table again. I placed myself back behind the three feet of mahogany where I'd slung so many drinks for years. Though there was no way to know it at the time, I'd be bartending for another two years before I could put it behind me for good.

But still, there was a silver lining. Though it may not have paid off for another fifteen years, this was the period when, despite the fact that I'd met my wife while working the bar and had many a laugh behind many a bar, I wanted out of bartending for good. I went back to *Backstage* magazine. Only this time, I wasn't looking for posts about gigs, I was posting an ad. I began to teach an acting class and coach young actors. While it didn't make me much money, it inspired me. And with the benefit of hindsight, I can now see that the joy I got from teaching turned out to be the seed that eventually grew into the *10,000 NOs* podcast in 2017 and now, into this book that you're reading.

Top Three Takeaways

1. Risk is necessary. Without it, you can't leave your house, let alone accomplish any dreams.

2. Taking a risk implies that you can lose just as easily as win.

3. Contrary to popular belief, you can't have it all. When choices work out, they feel good. When they don't, you need to remind yourself that this isn't the end of your story and continue to take risks.

CHAPTER

6

Perseverance

"Keep 'em choppin', keep 'em choppin', lalalalalala!!!!"
—*Coach Hurley, Freshman Football Coach,*
John Jay High School

You've now heard enough stories to understand why, when I am asked to speak to soon-to-be graduates of MFA (Masters of Fine Arts) acting programs in Los Angeles, I describe my job as "being told 'no' for a living." It usually elicits a chuckle from at least a few of the graduates, but hearing my stories about the intricate and unique ways in which I've been pounded by "the business," it starts to sink in that they need to prepare themselves for a life of rejection if they are really going to carry on as professional actors. Perhaps the adjective that most encapsulates the qualities inherent in any actor who has lasted more than a decade is "perseverance."

Perseverance Is for Everyone

I don't believe that perseverance is just for actors. *Merriam-Webster's Dictionary* defines perseverance as "continued effort to do or achieve something despite difficulties, failure or opposition: STEADFASTNESS." My personal definition of perseverance has always been "the ability to go on, when the going gets tough."

As such, perseverance applies to every relationship and every activity in which we engage throughout our lives, from our kids to our jobs to our relationships. Because the things that matter most to us are never going to be perfect right off the bat, or ever, for that matter. Which is why we need to practice *follow through* when things don't go as planned.

Had I been able to Google "statistics for actors" when I was considering this profession back in the mid-1990s, there's a good chance I wouldn't be writing this book right now. If I had *really* examined the cauldron into which I was considering jumping, I might've run the other way. Here's just one quote I would have seen:

> "The statistics are *terrifying* … many actors will admit that there are some roles where payment arrives, *not in the form of money*, but in *opportunity* or *experience*."
> —Alice Vincent, *"More than Half of Actors Are Under Poverty Line,"* The Telegraph, *January 17, 2014*

Luckily, I didn't research the statistics. Nor did I listen to everyone who tried to talk me out of it. When people asked me if I had a Plan B, I would tell them that a back-up plan meant that, on some level, I thought I was going to fail. I had my doubts, but when I expressed them to my cousin, who worked as a New York City schoolteacher by day while helping to raise three kids and gigging with his guitar over 200 nights a year to bolster his music career, he said, "You're 22. Try it for three years. If you get nowhere, you can always go get a real job." That was the spirit that got me up and running. About a year later, in the summer of 1995, Ron Howard's *Apollo 13* came out and I adopted the phrase that Ed Harris delivered with perfection, "Failure is not an option."

I realize that the quote atop this chapter may appear as if it is just some sounds coming out of the mouth. But, as overly simple and potentially "meathead-ish" as it may sound, there are pearls of wisdom to be put toward our entire existence contained in that one little expression. The manner in which it was delivered to us repeatedly by our coach throughout my freshman football season is also of note. In order to mine that wisdom, we need to break it down.

"Keep 'em choppin'" refers to a football player's feet continuing to move through the whistle that ends each play, during which time the player continues to block an opponent. This is all an attempt to free up a lane for the running back to reach the opposing team's end zone and carry the ball across the goal line for a touchdown. "Chopping," in this context, means to keep one's feet moving up and down incessantly, digging one's cleats into the ground over and over in an attempt to move a defensive player backward. The "lalalalalala" part of the phrase was delivered with great volume and gusto as it served to motivate and inspire players to move opponents who were sometimes twice their size and would require every ounce of effort. This quote would be ineffective if delivered without energy as it is supposed to mimic the sound of an engine pumping. It's worth noting that people often say "lalalalalala" while plugging their ears if someone nearby is attempting to tell them something they would prefer not to hear. There is an aspect of *not thinking* inherent in this command.

"And everyone that told me to go screw myself, I didn't make a note of it … Funny enough, by only recognizing my positives, I was up to [five times more deals closing]."

—*Steve Sims, Founder/CEO, Bluefish; Author,*
Bluefishing: The Art of Making Things Happen

Not thinking, while often considered a negative action that one should avoid, can be employed in certain circumstances to great effect, particularly in the pursuit of a predetermined goal. In football, there is a lot of thought about *whom* one should be blocking on any given play and *in which direction* one should move them. Contrary to an outsider's perspective, the game of football contains much strategy and specificity. These are *huge* aspects of the game, even on a freshman level. Despite the fact that it may look like a bunch of people grunting and hitting one another, football, in many ways, can be thought of as a live-action, human chess match. But once you've determined the *who* and the *where*, thought is no longer needed. From that point on, tenacity and perseverance wins. You don't need to be the fastest or the strongest, particularly in high school, in order to be effective. If you can stick to your assignment through the whistle, which signals the end of each play, you can be an integral part of any team. And that's all I did.

I took Coach Hurley's teachings to heart because, despite *loving* football, my unique combination of slow, skinny, and weak didn't bode well for my NFL dreams. Luckily, I was given more than my share of hustle and drive at birth. Somehow, I always had the ability to stay in the game even after disastrous results, a skill that I've used over and over as an actor. That said, as much as I tried, there were many times when all I got for my efforts were disastrous results.

One such instance came at the end of my first year on the varsity team, as a junior. Prior to that year, I played tight end, an offensive position well-suited to my lean build. I played defensive end as well, which seemed logical. But junior year, despite my lean build, I had been shifted to right tackle on the offensive side of the ball. The build of a prototypical tackle is closer on the spectrum to that of a sumo wrestler. I, on the other hand, looked more like a string bean; standing at six foot two, I only weighed about 160 pounds soaking wet. The fact that Coach Hurley's mantras still floated through my brain two years later was essential. I would need all the heart and energy I could muster to be effective in this new position.

> "Instead of being a victim in my life, I'm going to become the superhero of my own story and I'm gonna take this and I'm gonna use this and I'm gonna have it help me achieve something that I think is really special."
>
> —*Siri Lindley, World Champion Triathlete*

Despite my lack of size, my varsity coach, Jim Capalbo, shockingly ended up giving me more playing time than most of my fellow junior-year teammates that season. Ability-wise, I probably didn't belong on the field, but Coach liked my attitude, so throughout the season I would substitute in on offense and defense periodically. Our starters at the tackle and defensive end positions were two seniors, both of whom were not only two inches taller than me, but also outweighed me by a good 50 or 60 pounds each. So, while I loved getting opportunities to play, and I'd like to believe I was well-liked by my teammates, I was also cognizant of what we were sacrificing as a team every time I took the field.

Sometimes Life Is Going to Pancake You

At the end of the year, the larger of our two giant seniors went down with an injury and I was called up. I was told I'd be starting both ways in our Bowl Game, which was a big deal for a junior on that team. I wish I could finish this story with a glorious ending, but this tale turned out quite the opposite. I'm proud of what I did that day, firing off the ball with vengeance in an attempt to make up for my lack of size against the 6-foot, 4-inch, 230-pound monster lined up across from me. But there is one particular play that will always stick out in my mind from that game, like a recurring nightmare of helplessness. The guy I went up against all game in the cold mud was a senior on the opponent's team and he was not only large, but strong and quick, too. And while my frame put up a valiant fight, there was at least one play where heart was outmatched by physics.

Stopped on three downs and forced to punt, we were hoping to at least pin the opposing team deep into their territory. Unlike run-blocking, where a lineman fires off the line and tries to push their opponent backward, punt-blocking is more passive. When the ball is snapped, the offensive lineman, my position on this play, moves backward slightly while staying in a ready position. This allows the defensive lineman to fire off the ball and smash into him with less opposition than usual. And, if that defensive lineman outweighs the offensive lineman by 70 or so pounds, he has a chance to "pancake" him, flattening him out as he runs him over. This Goliath fired off the line at me. I met him with resistance and dug my cleats in, but the muddy field beneath me may as well have been ice. As I "kept 'em choppin'," he proceeded to plow me backward as though I were a moveable blocking sled on skates. I remained between him and our punter for about five yards until my cleats dug in and caused me to stop dead in my tracks, at which point he pancaked me.

I can't be sure that my memory is accurate as, at that point, I was flat on my back, but I believe that after said pancaking, he somersaulted, then popped up gracefully just in time to block our punt. The other team recovered the ball and eventually marched down the field and scored.

To say that I was solely responsible for our loss would be an overstatement, but this play certainly does not belong on my high school football highlight reel. Regardless, it did not keep me from playing football again. As we used to say: get up, dust yourself off, and get back in the game. My senior year we went 8 and 2 for the season. Regardless of a loss or a terrible game, we did not quit or give up. Instead, we persevered.

> "I try to teach my kids to be unoffendable ... to take a problem, take an issue, find the good side of it and laugh at it. And go through it with the muster you need to get through that next storm. Things will always get better on the other side."
> —*Matt Long, Ironman Triathlete, Author,*
> The Long Run: A New York City Firefighter's
> Triumphant Comeback from Crash Victim
> to Elite Athlete

Likewise, the final game of my high school lacrosse career, where we lost in the sectional finals to the eventual state champion despite being ahead at halftime, was an emotional event for me. The frustration and sadness were not just from the loss, but from the fact that my coach pulled me in the second half to give time to an underclassman, forcing me to watch the end of my high school lacrosse career from the sidelines. It was not only maddening, but humiliating. It left a bad taste in my mouth for my high school coach and it dampened the end of that year for me. But it did not stop me from trying out for the team when I arrived at Boston College. If we stopped every time we had a setback or suffered humiliation, we would never get anywhere. The truth is that those humiliations feel huge to *us*, but no one else usually remembers them. I recently recounted this story to a few of my old teammates and they barely remembered me being pulled in that second half. They were too caught up in their own dramas. Today, in interviews, I'm never asked what it felt like to be pancaked on a punt play or pulled from my final high school lacrosse game, but I've often been asked what it was like to play a sport at the Division I level. What a shame it would have been if I had quit before I had that opportunity.

Many times, when we berate ourselves for "failing," we realize after some time that that perceived failure was actually the steppingstone to a much larger success. While there are many parallels to these sports stories in my acting career, of carrying on in spite of how difficult an endeavor's challenges might be, the experiences that have cut the deepest for me are not necessarily from withstanding long hours on a grueling set. Many people in other fields, and huge stars in my own, share war stories of working in terrible conditions or trying to remain awake on the job after months of work without a good night's sleep. While I have a few of those, too, my toughest task has always been facing the abyss of unemployment as well as the emotional rollercoaster of near misses. In an industry where jobs can be won or lost on the whims of an executive's mood or any number of factors outside of my control, I have leaned heavily on a mantra of perseverance: "Just keep putting one foot in front of the other," and do not walk on that hill!

Is Your Biggest Break a Few Doors Down the Hallway?

There are too many harrowing stories from my career to fit in this book, but perhaps the one that emphasizes more than most the need to go on in spite of pain and heartache begins with, of all things, a soap opera. My agent called me with an audition for a series regular role on *As the World Turns*. This was not my dream job, but *any* job that was willing to consistently pay me to *act*, when my income came almost exclusively from bartending, was welcome. Just prior to the initial audition, I had gone through a breakup and spent the weekend preoccupied with its fallout. By the time I went in for the casting director, I was much less prepared than usual. In an ironic twist, my attitude of not caring much about the actual audition turned out to be the thing that helped me. When I went into the room, the casting director asked how I was but never peeled his eyes from his computer. The breakup still front of mind and not having the energy to fake it, I answered, "Not too good." This immediately caught his attention and brought him to my truth.

After a conversation about love, life, and relationships that went far deeper than usual audition-room chit-chat, he asked, "Are you sure you're okay to read?" I told him I'd give it a whirl and we read through the scene. Good acting is listening and reacting. And because I was emotionally depleted, that's all I had the energy to do. By the time I left the room I had a feeling I was in the mix. My agent called later that day and confirmed it. I was brought in for a callback a day or two later. Then, after about three *more* rounds of auditions, I found myself on set in Brooklyn for a screen test. By that time, I had done a lot of plays and student films, but I was still inexperienced enough that just being on an actual set was surreal.

The way my business is set up, sometimes the closer you get to landing a job, the more you feel like you want it. It's a combination of competitive juices and also knowing that the ensuing financial reward could change your life drastically. So a lot of the work, in addition to the actual script work, is to keep one's

nerves in check. I did that and, despite the pressure-cooker environment, I felt like I'd nailed it.

Because it was down to only me and two other actors, the
vibe from my screen test had me convinced that I was going to
have a good paying job and would be able say goodbye to bartending. But after a few long days, and the dream of steady paychecks,
I got the call from my agent that it wasn't going any further for
me. There was an initial surge of anger, and a desire to put my fist
through a plate-glass window. That lasted for a brief moment, but
then I just felt *empty*, depleted. It was an *awful* feeling, knowing
that all that work and excitement amounted to absolutely nothing
and that, the following day, I'd be back to square one.

Much like the embarrassment in my sports stories, there is
a blow to the ego in this kind of rejection. But it's also more than
that. There is a bleakness and a feeling of being overwhelmed
that occurs when something *feels* like an alignment of the planets that will lead toward a change in destiny but ends up being
nothing. With each rung on the ladder that is climbed, the internal narrative shifts to make sense of it and, in order to give ourselves the best shot at getting the job, we speak as though the best
possible outcome has already occurred. It's hard not to imagine
a whole life laid out before you with that job playing an integral role. But when the rug is pulled from beneath you just as
quickly as it appeared, it can lead to a depressive slump. It's in
these slumps where even the best men and women have their
mettle tested.

"When the judge just … smacked it down like that,
just … '20 years.' Reality really kicked in as they started
cuffing me up, ya know, my family's starting to cry. I was
like, 'All right, this is the reality of the situation. I'm
gonna make every day count. There's not gonna be one
day I look back on and think, why didn't I use this time

more effectively?' I'm gonna change my life and I'm gonna help other people change their lives."

—*Rob Grupe, Owner/CEO, Twice Bitten CrossFit*

Reminding myself that failure is just built into the game, I chose to continue playing despite my bruised ego. As I had done in sports, I picked myself up, dusted myself off, and got back in the game. Anyone who has played basketball, even in a pickup game, knows that you can't score unless you continue to take shots at the hoop, even when those shots bounce off the backboard like bricks. This particular decision to persevere paid off not too long after my *As the World Turns* experience, when I went through another grueling series of callbacks for a pivotal role on a different show: *The Sopranos*. And, as fate would have it, my audition yielded more fruit than that of the soap opera screen test. I got the gig.

This is no disrespect to the many great actors who got their starts on soap operas or those who make their living doing soaps currently. It is hard work that comes with challenges that can make an actor much better at their craft if they approach it with the right attitude. But, for me, *The Sopranos* set me on a different path than I would have been on had I landed the soap role. It helped lead the way to all of the other prestigious projects I've been fortunate to be a part since. And getting it was a stroke of luck that I couldn't have seen coming the day my agent told me I wasn't getting the soap. Had I folded after that initial "failure," had I said, "I'm no good, I'm just gonna quit," I never would've known the possibility that the biggest break of my career was only a few doors down the hallway.

You never know what the next page in your book will bring, but you need to remind yourself that your story is not over. Wherever you may be, whether in a good position or bad, there is only one thing that you control: your reaction to the events of your life. If your attitude is poor when bad things occur or the outcome is not what you expected, it is likely that when good things happen you will squander them. The expression "Wherever you go, there you are" is a warning: get your head right now and you will have more opportunities. None of us are immune from setbacks, but all of us are capable of overcoming them.

Top Three Takeaways

1. No matter who you are or what you do, perseverance is as important for you to learn as anything.
2. You cannot choose what will happen to you, but you can choose how you will react to it.
3. Your story is not over. Just beyond your current struggle is something better.

CHAPTER

7

Reframing

"Maybe that was a gift that my father gave me, from a young age I got burdened with so much. I hated him for a long time because of it. But now as I've gotten older, I use him a lot in my work. He is my darkness. He is a part that really completes me, as a person, as an artist."

—*Sarah Shahi, Actor* (The L Word, Person of Interest)

The way in which we frame experiences and people throughout our lives is possibly *the* most important factor in determining not only our success, but also our happiness and peace of mind on this earth. If I had to pick just *one* lesson from this book that I'd like you to walk away with, it is probably this. Because all of us, whether we're a Navy SEAL, an Academy Award–winning actor, or atop the Forbes Fortune 500 List, will experience loss, tragedy, defeat, and emotional emptiness at some point in our lives. That is a given because all of us are human. What will differentiate us, however, and the quality of our lives, is how we choose to *interpret* those experiences and thus, how we *respond* to them.

It's Not the Canvas, It's What You See
in the Canvas

I remember a time in elementary school when a black-and-white photocopy of a sketch was being passed around. When it was handed to someone for the first time, it was accompanied by the question, "What do you see?" Half the people would say it was a picture of an old lady. They'd point to her protruding chin and her bumped nose, her sad eyes looking downward, and the white kerchief that served almost like a hood. The other half of the people who looked at the photocopy came back with a drastically different description. They described a beautiful young woman, with a strong jawline and gorgeous cheekbones, exposing her exquisitely slender neck as she demurely turned away from the viewer. The only part of her face that was exposed was a long, curly eyelash and the tip of her petite and perfect nose. One picture, two drastically different descriptions. While this mental exercise fascinated me at the time, I had *no* idea just how much its principles would later become a part of my life.

One of my best friends from college, the same one who introduced me to his sky-diving friend from Chapter 5, is a highly regarded trauma surgeon in Boston. He is also a member of the Harvard Medical School faculty and, prior to that, served as a Navy SEAL. If you're wondering why I allowed such a slacker into my inner circle, I believe it was to keep me humble. Fortunately for me, this friend and I have been having in-depth conversations around the topics covered in this book for the nearly three decades since we met. One of the things I love, which he shared with me shortly after he made the transition from SEAL to doctor, is something he would do when invited to speak to various organizations and schools. He would project two huge lists on a screen behind where he stood. These lists were resumes, displaying contrasting accomplishments and failures of two drastically different potential candidates for some fictitious position. Going through the two different individuals' lists with the audience, he would ask them to help him figure out why one had failed so much while the other thrived.

One of the applicants, tragically, could never seem to grasp his goals. He wanted to be a fighter pilot, but eventually changed his mind. He wanted to play lacrosse in college, but despite being very athletic, he was cut before making the team. He had trouble focusing, which led him to quit many sports as a youngster, including gymnastics, because he wanted to "have a normal life." He was told by his college counselor, when asking for guidance in reaching medical school, that his extracurricular activities would not be enough to compensate for his mediocre grades, so he should give that dream up. In short, this candidate could be described as a loser.

On the other hand, the list of the second individual was astonishing. He had breakdanced for the Washington Redskins when he was only in sixth grade. He was a Delaware-Maryland-Virginia gymnastics champion before middle school. He got his varsity letter in football and lacrosse before choosing *not* to play Division I lacrosse in college so he could earn his tuition through the Navy ROTC program. He later chose to become a Navy SEAL and not only made it through their legendary training to receive his Trident, but eventually earned prestigious awards. Upon leaving the Navy, he coached his high school's lacrosse team and taught English literature while studying for his medical school entrance exams. He aced the exams, flew through med school, and was honored by the White House for his exemplary service during seven deployments in Afghanistan and elsewhere as the first doctor to also be called upon for his combat expertise. He later opened his own practice and became a member of Harvard Medical's faculty.

By this point, maybe you've guessed that the second individual is, in fact, my friend. But what makes him so different from that first candidate? Why has he succeeded where this other individual has failed? The answer is quite simple: he hasn't. That other individual is also my same friend. From a certain vantage point, even an American hero with a life story that reads like the screenplay from *Forrest Gump* can appear to be an abysmal failure.

This is true for all of us. *How we frame and interpret the events of our life* determines our destiny. The good news is that this skill can be taught. Just as the kids in my elementary class who saw the old woman in that sketch were able to discover the young lady once she was described to them, *you* can discover the heroism and victory in your own story if someone points out to you where it lies. Friend and past guest Toni Torres made her way out of extreme poverty in the ghettos surrounding Cleveland all the way to being a working actor in Hollywood. She reframed her entire life to prevent herself from ending up dead or selling drugs like so many of the kids with whom she grew up.

> "I went through this stage where I started saying my parents were in sales ... because they sold drugs."
>
> —*Toni Torres, Actor*

A few years back, I uttered a phrase to my wife that describes the action I partake in pretty much every day: *willful denial*. Let's break it down. According to *Merriam-Webster's Dictionary*, the definitions of these terms are as follows:

willful - adj., 1 - obstinately and often perversely self-willed
2 - done deliberately: INTENTIONAL
denial - n., refusal to admit the truth or reality of something
(such as a statement or charge)

I'm sure a psychologist would have a field day with me on this and point out the errors of my ways. But I'm not denying that what I do is a little insane. (In fact, if I set my sights on writing a second book, I'm going to call it *Crazy Enough*.) I believe that anyone who has ever achieved anything beyond a modicum of success could, from at least one perspective, be perceived as a little off their rocker. The very vision that creates art where there was once a blank canvas, or massive commerce where there once existed either inefficiency or a large gap between buyers and sellers, is full of willful denial. When a poet, novelist, or entrepreneur creates something that eventually wins them awards or massive amounts of money, they are being rewarded for refusing to look at what's in front of them as the only real option and, instead, creating something that no one else realized could exist. This is the same thing we must all do on a daily basis when faced with challenges that might otherwise stall us or, worse, derail us altogether.

Living with someone who engages in this behavior incessantly, as my wife has been forced—er, *chosen*—to do with me, might be enough to drive a person insane as well. This is why so many documentaries about individuals who changed the world in some way also turn their focus on the spouses and families of those individuals: the people in close proximity sometimes suffer from the shrapnel that disperses every time one of these grand visions implodes or comes crashing down to earth—or even succeeds beyond wildest expectations. What's possibly more infuriating for these supporters is that the person responsible for the thing that is crashing will rarely admit that the crash was a bad thing. I'm not suggesting that we don't examine the errors of our ways or analyze our past missteps in order to improve upon them. It should be obvious that post-execution assessments need to be made on a regular basis for us to get better. But it is also necessary to frame things with the sentiment that life happens *for us*, not *to us*, in order for us to maintain positive emotional engagement.

There's No Business Like Show Business

Let me give you some classic examples of this from my own life.

When the ABC series *Mistresses*, starring Alyssa Milano, told me after one episode that they wanted to bump me up from a guest star to a series regular, where I'd make exponentially more money, I was excited. Then I learned that they wanted to lock me into the show exclusively for the remainder of that season with no pay raise, and merely the *promise* of a series-regular position *if* the show got picked up for another season, which is never a sure thing. This sounded like a bait-and-switch so I said no, remained at my low price, and finished out the season without being tied to the show exclusively. All throughout that season, the creators told me that I was the soulmate to the woman across from whom I was playing and that they *needed* me for the duration of the show.

When *Mistresses* got picked up for a second season, I was invited to attend a party in Hollywood to celebrate. Even though it was a long drive and our young kids were home, I wanted to go. I wanted to celebrate with my castmates, and it was also smart business as I'd be getting the call about my new deal as a series regular probably within days after the party. We had some drinks and hugged each other, proud of the accomplishment. I wanted to ask about my deal, but of course that wasn't the right time or place. When a week went by, and then another, with no call, I pressed my agents and manager to call them and find out why there was a delay. It wasn't until we reached out that we heard the news: the network was being tight with money so they couldn't add a new series regular to the roster. I had to make a choice: tell them to go screw themselves unless they made me a series regular or do the show as a guest star again, for the reduced rate, because having a job was better than unemployment. Given our financial situation and young kids, I chose to continue as a guest star and worked hard to assuage my ego. The bold truth was that I felt burned and was pissed off. But what I told myself, and the world, was that I was happy to have a job and actually grateful that I wasn't locked in so I could go do other projects.

That last line sounds good, but as the second season continued and most of my time was spent on set or auditioning for other projects that ultimately didn't want me, its logic felt thin. Until, out of nowhere, I was asked to do a favor for a casting director (you'll hear that whole story in Chapter 15, Just Be a Good Person), and before I knew it I was telling *Mistresses* they had to shoot my scenes out before I left for New Orleans to be one of the main villains in *Hot Pursuit*, the first studio movie I'd ever booked. Don't get me wrong, I truly liked all of the producers on *Mistresses*, and I can look back now and know that their decision to not make me a series regular was not only *not* personal, but likely out of their hands and mandated by the network and studio. I'd be lying, though, if I didn't admit the sweet revenge I felt as they had to bend their schedule around mine to get my episodes in the can. My willful denial from the summer before had turned into truth.

"I would write, 'I'm gonna be in a commercial with
LeBron and Serena.' And I'd write it over and over and
… ends up, I was in a Nike commercial with LeBron
and Serena. It was the big Colin Kaepernick ad."
—*Charlie "Rocket" Jabaley, Entrepreneur, Speaker,*
Nike Athlete

I have followed this pattern so many times because the
nature of an acting career is that, even when things work out,
there is a shelf-life for most projects that is laughably short. For
this reason, rather than viewing the end of a job as downer, the
attempt is to view it as a new opportunity to reinvent oneself
with whatever project comes next. Sometimes that is easier said
than done, like when *Huge in France* was canceled by Netflix less
than a month after we became available for streaming, despite
rave reviews online and a bit of a cult fervor among comedy
folks in my industry. Shocked by their decision, and with no
choice but to move on, I quickly released it from my mind and
focused on the potential of *City on a Hill* becoming my new
home. Perhaps the situation that I'm most proud of reframing is
something that I did as a result of a major hiccup during my run
on ABC's *Scandal*.

Out of Work? Start a Podcast!

My run as Michael Ambruso on *Scandal* came literally out of
nowhere. But, as my brother used to jokingly say when we were
kids playing football in our basement and he'd stop me from a
touchdown, "The Lord giveth and the Lord taketh away." This
was definitely true for *Scandal* because, as easily as this one came
to me, the bottom dropped out on it at the most surprising time.
I was in Utah in 2016 close to wrapping filming on *Wind River*,
a feature film that eventually made a splash at Sundance and in

theaters, when I got a call from my manager. She told me that Shonda Rhimes (the creator of *Scandal*) wanted to "use me big time in the upcoming season." I was not under contract with the show so my work was subject to the whims of the scripts that came in, but a call like this was as close to a guarantee as one could get. Not only that, they were giving me specific dates. There would be 16 episodes that season, and they would halt production in the fall for Kerry Washington to have her baby and then resume and work through April of the following spring. It felt like a lock.

Later that year, I got an opportunity to move my family into a house close to where our kids go to school, but it meant doubling our monthly overhead. Knowing I had work coming, my wife and I were inclined to take the leap. I never did find out what changed the storyline of *Scandal* that season—perhaps it was the election that put Trump in office (because it's a show that takes place in and around the White House)—but somehow my "big-time" stint dropped to only three episodes. I was without work and that particular pilot season did not bode well for an actor of my type. In the wake of the #OscarsSoWhite movement, which protested the snubbing of several African American–led films that perhaps should have been in contention that year, many of the roles I may have been considered for in the past were now being cast with minorities. As an American interested in giving everyone an opportunity, I was happy to see this. But as the breadwinner in my household, I was out of work. I couldn't seem to get any potential employers' attention during that pilot season despite feeling good about my work in the audition rooms.

What I did with that disappointment, despair, and fear is probably my biggest source of pride to date. Naturally, it involved a classic "Del Negro Reframe." Instead of continuing to let the weight of all my rejections and lengthy periods of unemployment bog me down, as they had in the past, I decided to flip them on their head. Having discovered podcasts a year or two before,

I fell in love with the raw and authentic style of this audio-only medium where a listener could be a fly on the wall, hearing conversations between people to whom they otherwise might never gain access. I decided to take all of my "no"s, all of my rejections and failures that I tended to hide away from others and minimize in the hopes of appearing to be "fine," and turn them into my platform. The result, *10,000 NOs*, has been the most inspirational three years of my life, as of this writing. It has helped me to reconnect to the dreams that were in jeopardy of being snuffed out. It has also connected me to people around the world who have become as addicted as I am to these stories of resilience that I have been lucky enough to find and present.

In its first few years, the *10,000 NOs* podcast did not bring me financial reward, other than what I've received to write this book from a publisher I was introduced to through one of my guests. It has always, however, brought me something that may be more valuable than money—passion, purpose, and service. I firmly believe that these three assets will end up bringing me even more financial success someday, but it will truly be the side effect of the *real* gold. Service, passion, and purpose are the lifeblood that keeps me engaged and constantly striving, and are integral parts of any success I may achieve. When I become too caught up in my own drama, I am pulled out of it by notes from around the globe of people with tougher challenges than me. These notes express how listeners have been inspired by the stories of guests overcoming obstacles. In this way, my decision to reframe the aspect of my career that I hated the most ended up saving not only my career, but my soul. Had I continued down the worn path I'd been traveling, I might have burned out by now.

The adverse effects of any experience can be reversed by choosing to reframe the way those effects are perceived. I do not say this as though I have had to experience tragedies anywhere close to those of my guests or others I have read or heard about.

I say this because each inspiring comeback story I encounter, whether personally or from afar, has an element of reframing in it that allowed the comeback to happen. Try it for yourself, in situations as small as waiting on a long line for coffee or as big as the tragic loss of a loved one. It may not ease your pain immediately, but eventually it will open the door to potential recovery.

Top Three Takeaways

1. Depending on the vantage point from which you look, *anyone's* life story can appear tragic or heroic.

2. Anyone who has ever made a large impact on others could be perceived as being a little crazy from at least one person's perspective.

3. Adopt the mantra "Life happens *for* you, not *to* you." It will help you see *everything* as being on your side.

CHAPTER

8

Surrender

"I was done. I can't even tell you the level of despair. I was just done. I was like, 'I've hustled my whole damn life. And here I am, it's gone. Everything's gone.'"
—*Suzy Batiz, Founder/CEO, Poo~Pourri,* Forbes *Top 5 Female Self-Made Millionaires, 2018*

I talk a lot about grinding. I won't shut up about work ethic and hustle. But there is something that I've learned relatively recently that can *feel* like the opposite of hustle and grind, yet can result in great success: surrender. Surrender is a little different than relaxation and meditation, which you'll read about later. Surrender does not always wait for an invitation to join your life. It is a party-crasher. And, while surrender is not always something that is *welcome*, if it decides to show up, it can't be denied and generally can't be kicked out until it has run its course.

The Art of Fighting Without Fighting

When I was a kid, I loved Bruce Lee movies. One of my favorites was *Enter the Dragon*. The setup for Lee's character includes a scene in which a bully threatens him. Known for his fighting prowess, Lee's character was a magnet for such meatheads. Riding a boat across a harbor, surrounded by others who were eager to watch a bloody match, Lee accepts the challenge. But, he adds, they should fight on the attached lifeboat where there is more room. He gestures for the bully to climb onto the dinghy and the bully willingly goes, confident he can beat Lee regardless of *where* they fight. While bantering back and forth with all the onlookers waiting in anticipation, Lee nonchalantly unties the lifeboat from the main boat and it, with the bully on board, drifts away from the larger boat. The bully is furious but there's nothing he can do to get back to Bruce and the rest of the crowd. It is the perfect execution of Lee's patented "art of fighting without fighting." Sometimes surrender can bring victory to you quicker than anticipated, but usually that victory will come in a different form than you originally envisioned.

Surrender is generally associated with weakness and defeat, but when it comes to surrendering ourselves to the unknown, it requires a strength of character and self-possession that few can boast. When you surrender you are telling the world that your self-preservation is more important to you than maintaining whatever public persona you have carefully crafted. It means that you are willingly admitting defeat and not above being deemed a quitter. It does *not* mean, however, that you are admitting *permanent* defeat.

> "If they're stuck on the 'quitters never win, winners never quit' ... look at how many people who have quit things, even very publicly, who are people we definitely

consider winners. Michael Jordan: how many times did he quit and unquit? And he's arguably one of the biggest 'winners' in basketball of our time."

—*Lynn Marie Morski, Founder/CEO, Quitting by Design; Physician, Attorney, Speaker, Author, and lifelong quitter*

As I shared in Chapter 1, in college I had plenty of pain and feelings of being overwhelmed that led to my eventual shift to acting. Pain that brings us to our knees can come from anywhere without warning. Sometimes, a debilitating accident can cause physical pain and limitations that force us to surrender, regardless of how strong we may be. This happened to my friend and former *10,000 NOs* podcast guest Matt Long. A tough New York City firefighter, competitive marathon runner, and Ironman triathlete, Long was forced into the reinvention he eventually underwent by the limitations placed upon him after being run over by a bus.

The accident occurred as Long was riding his bike through Manhattan on his way to work. A young bus driver, with zero experience driving in the city, jerked his bus across three lanes of traffic without warning, pinning Long and his bike underneath. Long nearly bled out on the sidewalk as his bike was sawed from the undercarriage of the bus. Doctors gave him a 1% chance of survival. In an astounding comeback, Long recovered, got rid of the colostomy bag he was forced to wear for two years, and learned to walk again. If that weren't miraculous enough, he relearned how to run before willing himself to complete another New York City Marathon less than three years after the accident. He then regained his Ironman status by completing the grueling 2.2-mile swim, 110-mile bike, and 26.2-mile run under the allotted time in Lake Placid, New York, the following year. He now credits his accident as the source of everything that's good in his life today, particularly his wife and kids. But there was a time immediately after his accident when his outlook was far more bleak and hopeless.

> "The fire that burned inside me was out and I had no idea what my life was going to be like, what the future held. I knew I survived but I didn't know what kind of quality of life that I was going to lead. I led a life full of quality and it was taken away from me. And it took me a long time. When I was in this dark place and I saw no future I couldn't see past the external fixators that were coming through my chest to hold my pelvis together or the external fixator coming through my leg to keep my left leg together. Because I was basically cut in half and I couldn't see past that. And that's where things got dark."
>
> —*Matt Long, Author,* The Long Run

In a similar story, former Navy SEAL Jason Redman sustained injuries during a nighttime mission in Iraq when he and his platoon were ambushed. Injured, Redman recognized in the moment that he had to surrender, not to enemy forces but to the capabilities of his highly trained platoon. While Redman firmly believes that it is a fatal flaw for people to wait for a bad situation to fix itself without making an effort to "get off the X" themselves, even *he* acknowledges his surrender on that battlefield. Had his platoon not won the battle as he lay bleeding out, he never would have survived his nearly fatal wounds.

"I remember lying there thinking, 'This sucks. I can't move. I'm pinned down. I think I lost my arm.' So I'm thinking, 'You're gonna bleed out quickly.' And I knew from our training that our guys could not come get me. We have trained that in a fierce firefight, if someone gets wounded, you cannot run out to get them. The enemy will use it as a tactic. They'll wound someone on purpose to try to lure other people out there to get them. So I knew I had to wait. I had to be patient and just trust my guys to win that fight." Part of what evolved out of this experience is Redman's current role as author and speaker, in which he teaches others about responding to what he calls "life ambushes."

The "All Is Lost" Moment Is Not Only in Movies

Unlike Long and Redman's physical pain, what I experienced in Italy was emotional. It was the surrender to an emotional pain that friend and former podcast guest Suzy Batiz experienced when she, before creating and running her now-$500 million (as of 2019 when we spoke) company Poo~Pourri, went bankrupt for the second time. She explained to me that her surrender period was *the* thing that led to her breakthrough with Poo~Pourri after the age of 40.

After hearing the crank of the tow truck pulling her repossessed car out of her driveway as she literally lost everything, she lied to friends and family, telling them she had to move. This led to a four-year period where she didn't attempt to start any businesses, but instead sought refuge in seclusion, listening to angry music and painting: "I'm just painting my house. I'm just painting walls and just screaming with rage. Just going insane, the first time in my life I think I let myself actually feel what was happening."

At a Thanksgiving dinner, Batiz's brother brought up a project he'd been toiling with for a couple of years. He asked the table, "Can bathroom odor be trapped?" This one offhand question, in the midst of Batiz's period of surrender to the idea that she'd never attempt to create another business in her life, changed everything. "I'll never forget the feeling, it's like a zing up my arm ... everything goes into high-def and

I went, 'I can do that!'" As a hobby, Batiz had been working with essential oils for about 15 years. She had always been intrigued by natural products. "Everything just clicked. 'Oil floats on water.' It wasn't even as much of a rationale as it was literally like, 'I can do that!' I just saw it all."

It took her nine months, but after that dinner she went home obsessed with solving her brother's challenge. Everyone thought she was crazy. Today, when she speaks around the world she coaches entrepreneurs to stop seeking others' approval and follow their own "alive ideas." Her alive idea became an astoundingly successful company after she invested $25,000 of her own to begin it and then advertised it via word of mouth for the first six years. Her grit, determination, and perseverance helped it to grow exponentially, but it never would have been born had she not surrendered prior to its inception.

My experience in Italy, while external because it was incited by a breakup, felt more *internal*. My panic attacks, exacerbated by the breakup, were really the result of years of internalizing aspects of my parents' failing marriage, unspoken sibling differences, and schisms within myself without expressing them outwardly. Regardless of the root cause, my *reaction* to the pain was to surrender. I surrendered the persona and facade I had created up until that point, even while I was feverishly scrambling to understand all of the thoughts and emotions that had exploded from within.

Rather than continue to be ruled by my former mandate of showing up to class, like the "good boy" I always told myself I was, I surrendered to the overwhelming feelings that were threatening to sink me. I chose, instead, to skip class so I could pour my heart into my journal for eight to ten hours a day. It was anything but restful, and yet it was necessary if I was going to find peace. I was racing against the clock to unravel complex feelings inside me before their twisted mass suffocated me.

The overall effect of this intense period, particularly when I view it in retrospect, was that I pulled away from many of my previous associations and eventually focused myself on new ones, sending my life in a new direction. It is worth repeating that this process did not complete itself overnight. The rumblings of it began a few months prior to my trip overseas, in the spring of 1992. And while the most intense part of it took place over a one-month period while I was abroad that summer, I was still experiencing the fallout in the late fall after I had returned to the United States, when I finally quit the lacrosse team. *Maybe* you could say the following spring, when I did my first play, was the beginning of my new phase, but there were still many parts of my new self that continued to fall into place over the next several years.

> "I've learned how to let go more, and I'm not saying I've mastered this, but I've learned how to let go more and be in that state where things are coming to me with less effort than I used to think was necessary. And to not have that only happen at the end of a long period of exhaustion and suffering."
>
> —*Mike Boyle, Psychotherapist, PTSD Specialist*

I mention this time frame because many people will write in to the podcast saying something along the lines of, "I surrendered yesterday and I *still* don't see any signs that it was worth it. There's *nothing* on the horizon for me! Why did I give all of that up?!" Impatience can act like liquid poison, seeping into our psyche and causing us to second-guess ourselves repeatedly. Surrender takes a mountain of patience, and the universe has a funny way of knowing when we have *really* accepted our new circumstances. One of my favorite scenes in one of my favorite movies, *The Shawshank Redemption*, written by Frank Darabont, involves

Morgan Freeman's character, Red, who has been imprisoned for a lengthy sentence but is allowed to go before the parole board. Every year he explains to them how he has rehabilitated himself and why they should allow him to go free. In this scene, after many failed attempts over the years in which he has tried his best to give them the answer he thinks they want to hear, this is how he answers:

> RED : Rehabilitated? Well, now, let me see. You know, I don't have any idea what that means.
>
> PAROLE MAN : Well, it means that you're ready to rejoin society …
>
> RED : I know what you think it means, sonny. To me, it's just a made-up word. A politician's word, so that young fellas like yourself can wear a suit and a tie and have a job. What do you really want to know? Am I sorry for what I did?
>
> PAROLE MAN : Well, are you?
>
> RED : There's not a day goes by I don't feel regret. Not because I'm in here, or because you think I should. I look back on the way I was then, a young, stupid kid who committed that terrible crime. I want to talk to him. I want to try to talk some sense to him, tell him the way things are, but I can't. That kid's long gone and this old man is all that's left. I got to live with that. Rehabilitated? It's just a bullshit word. So you go on and stamp your forms, sonny, and stop wasting my time. Because to tell you the truth, I don't give a shit.

This scene exemplifies the way surrender works. We cannot trick the universe, or ourselves, into believing that we are ready to move on from whatever proverbial prison we are trying to escape. There is a purity of true surrender that must be reached before we are allowed to advance. It is one of the great contradictions of life: you cannot have something until you truly don't need it any more.

Grown Men Shouldn't Punch Walls

When it comes to my career, I don't need to go back very far to find a story about surrender. In December 2017, as the year drew to a close so did my run on Amazon's *Goliath*, starring Billy Bob Thornton. Perhaps filming my character's demise, when Danny Loomis plunged backward off a downtown Los Angeles rooftop to avoid being killed by his assailant after having his ear cut off, was a glimpse of what was to come of my career in the following few months. That incredible work experience, with artists and storytellers I truly respected, had me on a high from which I quickly slipped down into what felt like a cavernous gorge of unemployment.

If the unemployment wasn't enough to snuff me out on its own, I gave it some help. With the aid of a little alcohol, I made a boneheaded decision to punch a wall repeatedly. Not the hollow part of the wall, the part with a stud beneath it. In my mind, at the time, it was a passionate display to my wife of just how ready I was to prove "all the naysayers" wrong. For the record, our kids were both out at sleepovers, so at least they did not witness their father's idiocy. If this book is a compilation of all the mistakes I've made and the trials and errors of mine that can serve as guideposts for you to make better choices, then this is Exhibit A.

You know you've screwed up when, the following day, your hand hurts so badly you need to sit in the sand nursing it rather than partake in a beautiful day's surf session. The mistake is compounded even more when, later in the afternoon, your hand has swelled so much that it barely fits into your baseball mitt and the subsequent game of catch with your ten-year-old son is so painful that your eyes are filled with tears every time you catch one of his throws. Thank God, when I was persuaded the next morning to go to Urgent Care, I was able to tell the medics that both of my kids were out of the house when I committed this dumb act. That did not stop them from ogling me as though I was guilty of domestic violence, nor did it stop them from delivering the news that I had fractured my fourth metacarpal, also known as a boxer's fracture. That's a generous nickname for this considering a *real* boxer doesn't hit inanimate objects that can't hit back.

So there I was, out of work, unable to play baseball with my son or go on the trampoline with my daughter, and sporting a big, fat, maroon cast that wrapped around my entire wrist, half of my thumb and my entire pinky and ring finger. There was no hiding it. Everywhere I went, people would ask what happened. I considered making up some story about it being from a skiing accident or a boxing class, but ultimately I decided to surrender to it. If I was going to be honest with myself, I had to admit that this was the result of being a man who cares deeply about his craft and his career, and is painfully aware of how short he has fallen from the goals he had as a young actor. Despite having just finished the best job of my career, auditions were bearing no fruit and it felt like nothing had changed. This bonehead move just hurt my chances of employment even more because very few roles call for a moron sporting a big, doofy maroon cast. But the surrender to the truth of my actions, to not only myself but anyone who asked, ended up leading to my salvation.

I think I'm pretty straightforward with people, but when you start telling near-strangers that your 45-year-old self broke your hand punching a wall, it is a new level of exposure. It forced me to confront parts of myself that I'm not proud of and don't like very much. Several very generous fathers my age tried to lessen my discomfort upon hearing my tale, admitting that they had done the same thing. When I pressed them, however, and asked how old they were at the time, the age range that shot back was between 18 and 22. That only served to further solidify my stupidity and immaturity. But when you face this kind of shortcoming in yourself, over and over, day in and day out, eventually you accept yourself. You start to think, "Yes, I was dumb. But it doesn't define me."

Take Your Medicine and the Cure Will Find You

And sometimes, as eventually happened to me, the universe or God, depending on your beliefs, comes to your aid and throws you a bone after you've taken your medicine like a champ, much the way Red was granted his freedom once he finally accepted his guilt and took responsibility for his actions. After a dismal pilot season and a multitude of self-tapes, on which I tried to convince myself the cast would actually help, I found myself still looking for work that June. That was when the audition that led to the performance which got me the most individual attention of my career thus far came hurtling through the universe and landed in my lap.

Out of nowhere, I auditioned for the Netflix comedy series *Huge in France*. The role was that of Jason Alan Ross and the first time I read the material, despite finding it incredibly funny, I thought there was absolutely no way I would get it. On the page,

Jason was 30 years old, blond, buff, and not the sharpest knife in the drawer. That last part may not have been a stretch, but physically I wasn't right at all. I was nearly 46, dark-haired, and lean. It just didn't match. Luckily, though, on the *inside* I had just lived through *months* of Jason-like experiences. As I first recounted in Chapter 4, Jason was an actor, almost incessantly out of work, very proud and defensive of his dedication to his craft. *According to him*, a method actor. His girlfriend, who was also "employing" Jason by paying for his gas and cell phone bills in exchange for mentoring her teenage son through the paces of modeling and weight-training, did *not* view his acting with the same pride as Jason. In short, this guy was a down-on-his-luck loser with a big heart. On second thought, I was *perfect* for it!

One of the things I always say about acting is that *any* experience can be used. Really, that is another way of saying that if we surrender to any experience, we can eventually use it *for* us rather than having it work *against* us. Billy Joel was able to use what I'm sure was sometimes an excruciatingly frustrating experience working for paltry tips at a Long Island piano bar as a young musician to help him write the song for which he is most famous. In the case of *Huge in France*, despite a rushed schedule that lacked a surplus of prep time, my previous several months' surrender to my own desperation as an actor, combined with the diet and exercise regimen I explained in detail in Chapter 4, proved to be all the prep I needed.

Sadly, the series was canceled after one season, but that didn't completely erase my memory of when Netflix representatives, having watched a cut of the season for the first time, reached out to my representatives to tell them they'd be getting behind me for an Emmy campaign for my individual performance. Once the season was canceled, that never happened, but at least *I* know that my work didn't go totally unnoticed. I suppose I owe Netflix a thank-you—after all, they just added another "no" to my pile of 10,000 as well as a few sentences to this book. It's very simple: I can get mad and punch another wall, or surrender to it and have faith that this "no" will one day lead to a future Emmy campaign that ends with a "yes."

Top Three Takeaways

1. Surrender is not always welcome, but if it comes, you have no choice but to accept it.
2. You will only break free of your current prison when you admit to your part in why you're there in the first place.
3. *Any* experience can be used once you've surrendered to it and acknowledged it.

CHAPTER

9

Transformation

"So when I went to my artists and my business partners and I said that I wanted to retire they were confused. I said, 'I'm gonna be an athlete.' 'What does that mean, Charlie? 29 years old, 300 pounds, you're gonna be an athlete?' 'Yes. Because that was my dream that I buried when I was a little kid.'"

—*Charlie "Rocket" Jabaley, Entrepreneur, Speaker, Nike Athlete*

One of the most inspiring things about hosting a podcast about resilience is sitting face to face with individuals who have transformed their lives, and the lives of those around them, in dramatic fashion. While each chapter in this book touches upon various aspects of surviving and thriving, the underlying theme is really that of transformation. At its core, transformation is about adapting and allowing aspects of ourselves that are no longer serving us to die while simultaneously cultivating emerging aspects of self to move us in new directions. By transforming ourselves, we give ourselves access to that which we previously may not have even realized was available to us.

The Caterpillar, the Cocoon, and the Butterfly

The transformation of a caterpillar into a butterfly is an awesome feat of nature. Such a metamorphosis reflects the potential for change in all of us. The fact that a living being can go from being a hairy, 16-legged furry creature that inches along almost imperceptibly by contorting its rotund body with extreme effort and transform into a multicolored, intricately patterned, lithe being capable of flight is cause for awe and optimism. Many people go through their entire lives convincing themselves that they don't have the potential for that kind of change, or *any* change in some instances, for a variety of reasons. At the root of every one of those reasons is fear. It is through the surrender process I discussed in the previous chapter, and embracing the fear of the unknown, that we can emerge from our own cocoons and transform ourselves into what we always hoped to be.

For simplicity's sake, I'd like to break those who fear change and the potential for transformation into three groups. The first group, despite seeing examples of change all around them, do not believe that change is possible for *them*. The second group, even if they believe change is *possible* for them, complain that they do not *have access* to people with the techniques, both physical and psychological, to guide them to what they need to do in order to change. In today's day and age, using lack of access as an excuse to avoid change gets thinner by the minute with the abundance around us—not to mention what's at our fingertips just by clicking a link. In most cases, that is exactly what it is: *an excuse*. The third group of people believe that change is *possible* for them and that they *have access* to resources and people with techniques to help them change, but they still don't act on that belief or knowledge, because they *fear* the feelings that would ensue if they actually tried their best and still failed to reach their goal.

I must admit that I have been in all three of these camps at one time or another, and still find myself in them at times. Luckily, with a lot of work, I'm finding myself increasingly capable of positive change. But I have by no means graduated from this struggle. If you look at my story of physical transformation in Chapter 4, Discipline and Training, I mentioned the reason that story is noteworthy is because I had *tried* to transform my body so many other times in the past and failed. It is much easier to look around at high achievers and tell yourself that they are just lucky because they "have it all." It's not true, but it's easier than paying painstakingly detailed attention to your own actions and changing them where necessary.

And that's what must be done in order to optimize your results and achieve whatever it is that you're after. So, if you're looking for an *easy* way to change and attain everything you've ever wanted, I'm afraid you're out of luck. Instead, let me give you a tip I learned from a *master* of transformation, former *10,000 NOs* guest Don Saladino.

Saladino is known for transforming the bodies of some of the biggest names in Hollywood. In preparing them to play superheroes, he has helped actors like Hugh Jackman and Ryan Reynolds become Wolverine and Deadpool, respectively. He helped Blake Lively get back in fighting shape after she gave birth twice, and helped Liev Schreiber believably kick butt as Ray Donovan. In fact, when Blake Lively showed up early for her usual workout with Saladino, I was able to ask her if he

follows all of the principles he had just told me he uses. Here's
what she had to say:

> "He really understands the person he's training and
> their personal needs. So, beyond what your fitness
> goals are, he understands what's important to you. So
> you don't feel like, 'I'm gonna come in here and I'm
> gonna have to give up everything I love in order to
> achieve my goals.' You feel like, 'I can do this. I can
> stick with it.' He trains everyone differently because
> everyone has different goals."
>
> —*Blake Lively, Actor,* The Town, Gossip Girl

While those famous names certainly help Saladino's cause in
terms of attracting more business, what he's most proud of, and
what Lively made a point of mentioning, is the work he does with
people who are *not* famous, particularly those who are obese and
struggling to accomplish even basic physical tasks. Saladino told
me that one of the biggest factors in determining not only one's
ability to transform, but also one's ability to maintain said transformation, was doing *less*. He shared that most people come to
his gym, excitement in their eyes, willing to do *whatever it takes*.
They train every day, all day, and weigh their food down to the
gram. And, while this may be what Saladino does with his superstars after they've already been in a routine with him for a long
time and worked up to this load, it can spell death to the average
person's training regimen.

Saladino preaches that "If you drink four glasses of wine
every Friday night . . . just start out by limiting yourself to three."
He maintains that this "easy tweak" is not so hard to pull off. The
approach of gradual adjustments rather than going cold turkey
is intended to build confidence. Confidence builds excitement.
Excitement builds energy. Energy boosts daily routines. Higher

quality daily routines will produce better results. Better results will build confidence, and so on and so on. Using Saladino's principles, clients find themselves in an upward spiral that actually *builds* their momentum as they come closer to their goals rather than burning them out. And because the changes are made incrementally, they tend not to fall apart as quickly as the person who went from flab to six-pack in 45 days.

> "It's like the New Year's resolution. People dive into this stuff and they feel like it's all or nothing. People don't want to hear that sometimes the best approach is to take a long time. When you hear these people say, 'Oh, the six-week program ...' Can it work? Sure. But look at all the people who weren't able to hold onto it."
>
> —*Don Saladino, Strength Coach, Entrepreneur*

Yes, Saladino admits, people will sometimes take a step back after taking two steps forward. But this gradual approach to change can guard clients against major setbacks. When someone focuses on these minor changes more than worrying about how their transformation appears to *everyone else*, they eventually look in the mirror and find a butterfly staring back at them where a caterpillar once stood.

There Are No Small Parts, Only Small Actors

An obvious topic for an actor to cover when discussing transformation is the process of transforming oneself for a role. When you look at chameleons like Gary Oldman, Christian Bale, or Sam Rockwell, with their almost supernatural abilities to appear unrecognizable from themselves or their past roles, acting transformations can look like magic to an outsider. But, just as with physical transformations, when you break them down you realize that they are simply the result of very pragmatic and actionable choices that, compounded by time and aided by other professionals, add up to something that *appears* to be otherworldly. Actually, there is a bit of "other-world magic" that usually shows up in the best instances, but only gets the invite *after* all the hard work has been done.

I am fortunate enough to be acquainted with Sam Rockwell. When his name comes up, the comments I hear from moviegoers generally include astonishment at his transformational overhauls from role to role. While it's easy to just pass Rockwell off as "naturally gifted" or "lucky to get the roles he gets," that is not the whole story. Of course, he has gifts, which is why his performances for his recent turns in *Vice*, *Fosse/Verdon*, and *Three Billboards in Ebbing, Missouri* scored him an Oscar nomination, an Emmy nomination, and an Oscar win for Best Supporting Actor, respectively. But he also has an *insane* work ethic, and there is a focus and incremental transformation that takes place over time as a result of it.

> "It has rigor in it. It has discipline and rigor. It's not just show up and let's see what happens. [This method] makes you responsible. And it really puts into the body, through practice, practice, practice, practice this thing that the work eventually becomes inevitable."
>
> —*Terry Knickerbocker, Acting Coach*

Much like Jay Ferruggia's advice when I asked him to help me transform my body for *Huge in France*, making good *choices* is what separates the masters from the masses, regardless of one's chosen profession. Jay's laser-sharp guidance on my originally scattered goals narrowed my focus and encouraged me to only change one thing at a time. Rockwell begins his approach in the same way, starting slow and building up from there. My friend

Chris Messina invited me to read David Mamet's *American Buffalo* with him and Sam because Rockwell was preparing for a run of the play on Broadway in the spring of 2020. Even though it was only November 2019, Rockwell had already spent a lot of time with the script.

Reading with talents like Rockwell and Messina is always a pleasure. What is important for the purposes of *this* chapter, though, was Rockwell's relationship to the material. He knew that he was still light-years away from understanding his character the way he would understand him months later when the show opened. He expressed anxiety about reading it before we began. And yet, once we started, even at that early stage, his particular take on the character and the slow pace he took with his dialogue helped me to hear the play in a new way, despite having read it many times and seen multiple productions of it.

As good as it was, though, Rockwell stopped at one point to talk about the danger of letting a play this good *make our choices for us*. Mamet's rhythm and language is so delicious, it is tempting to spit it out fast so it *sounds* good, even though the actor uttering the words may not really know what he is saying. Conversely, by slowing down and mining for greater understanding of what matters to this character, and how he relates to *Sam*, Rockwell was able to connect on a personal level. He was aware that, for a true transformation to occur, the actor needs to bring him or herself to the role, including sometimes embarrassing inconsistencies and idiosyncrasies.

A Cobbled-Together "Career"

Compared to Sam Rockwell's storied career, I sometimes look at my own and lament that I've barely cobbled together something resembling a career by repeatedly taking on roles in which

I was miscast and doing my best to make something memorable and believable out of them. Despite this sometimes-depressing view of my own body of work, I have recently encountered a lot of strangers who have generously praised me by expressing how different I am in real life compared to how they perceived me in a particular role. These comments encouraged me to look back at my work with a less critical eye so I could celebrate a little more and self-bash a little less.

I was pleasantly surprised when I began to look at the spectrum of the roles I've played. With a few exceptions, each one of them, as I now reflect, is distinguishable from the others. There was the wet-behind-the-ears financial-advisor cousin to the wife of the mob boss on *The Sopranos*. There was the uncommonly competent advance man to the eventual President on *The West Wing*. I played a morally challenged sex worker who was using his body to make money by getting dirt on his employer's political opponent on *Scandal*. That character was eventually revealed to have a very sensitive and vulnerable side that was far from how he was perceived when he arrived on the scene. My characters in *Wind River*, *Goliath*, and *Chicago Fire* were different combinations of aggressive, manipulative, and largely corrupt individuals. I've touched on my *Huge in France* role, and then there's the "good cop" I'm currently playing on *City on a Hill*. As the captain of the Gang unit, my character leads with integrity and has his values straight. At least he does so far. Check back in after Season 2.

The point in bringing up a few of my roles is to provide examples of my own transformations that didn't always *feel* like transformations while I was making them. For each one of them I can remember a sense of feeling overwhelmed at the start, which doubled as excitement. But this sentiment was quickly replaced by solid steps toward transformation. In nearly every instance I wished I had more time to prepare, so I'd have to have at least a portion of self-forgiveness that it would never fully live up to what I wanted to do in my mind. Regardless, I would begin the work, knowing that each step I took would bring me closer to the character.

The way I work is to start by figuring out my jumping-off point with the character. As one of my acting coaches, Kim Gillingham, taught me to ask, "Why did this script hurtle through the universe and land in my lap right now?" That question encourages me to ask myself, what am I going through *right now* that can be infused into this character? And what can I learn from this character and his journey? These questions start to shift my awareness of the character from being *out there* to being a part of me.

This is not a book about acting specifically, so I will not go into depth about my own particular process. There is something to learn, however, from how actors can repeatedly transform themselves to the point where you can watch them in several different roles and believe, on some level, that they are someone else. The reason I brought up Sam Rockwell was to explain Saladino's point: small increments, over time, yield extraordinary results. Had Rockwell aimed for his opening-night performance from the first time he cracked open the play, he would never be able to *fully* transform. Likewise, if you constantly focus on aspects of your business that *appear* to be "official," like business cards or a website, but you fail to invest your time and efforts into the *substance* of what your business is about, the chances you'll fall short of the mark increase exponentially.

On the other hand, eventually all of those ancillary add-ons will be needed to complete the transformation. Just as most great businesses end up with business cards or effective websites, an actor needs the aid of other professional storytellers to really pull off their magic trick. Beginning with a great script, an actor is reliant on the material they are interpreting. This is why it's rare to see an Academy Award given for the portrayal of a character that was not interesting on the page to begin with. Likewise, an incredible wardrobe head or hair and makeup artist can take an actor's performance that is excellent on its own and push it over the top by applying the same specificity and care to the role as the actor has done. This goes for every aspect on a film or TV project, from the lighting, to the sets, to how the shots are framed and how the scenes are directed and later edited. There is a reason that when you've sat through a two-hour film that moves you to tears or belly laughs, it is followed by a list of credits a mile long. Just as the caterpillar cannot become a butterfly without the aid of sunlight, time, and the protection of a cocoon, no one can make a complete transformation on their own.

Breathing in Rarefied Air

I have been good friends with actor Chris Messina for over two decades, and our friendship has given me the benefit of hours and hours of conversations about the craft of acting. It has also given us the benefit of a very complex understanding of one another's work, because we have seen each other in so many different professional projects and personal crises over the years, as well as helped each other prepare for many of those projects. So when he was working on *Live by Night*, written and directed by Ben Affleck, and would call me from set to relay the latest chapter in our Actor's Journal, which exists in our heads only, he would end most conversations by saying, "This is rarefied air."

That reference was to the level of extreme talent on that set. Not only the names you may be familiar with, like Affleck, but other masters of their craft, like three-time Oscar-winning cinematographer Robert Richardson and Costume Designer Jacqueline West, who has been nominated for three Oscars, among others. In addition to the unbelievable amount of preparation Messina did for the role, including adding over

40 pounds of fat to his frame, he felt like he was in great hands with everyone who brought their own level of expertise to his portrayal. Even still, the film ended up being a disappointment at the box office. When that happens, people tend to write the whole project off, but it doesn't take away from all of the hard work by top craftspeople that went into it. Yes, even movie stars like Ben Affleck cannot escape their 10,000 "no"s.

While every one of my roles has relied upon, and benefited from, help from others, two specific instances come to mind. The first is the help I received from our technical advisor on the feature film *Wind River*. While my role in *Wind River* only required a little more than a week on set, the majority of that work revolved around a massive shootout in the snow, including my character and another character riddling each other with bullets before both dying. Luckily, we had an ex-Army Ranger to advise us on the technical aspects of shooting and warfare. Most people assume an actor takes all of their direction from the director, but in this case, the film's immensely talented writer-director Taylor Sheridan had many more things to worry about than my particular ability to handle a gun. While Sheridan was very helpful, I also spent a lot of time picking the brain of our advisor, to the point where we have continued the friendship to this day. Technically, he showed me how to load and reload my Glock in a quick and seamless fashion while under duress. We did it over and over again. I also spent hours asking him about his own combat experiences and one particular story he shared gave me incredible insight into the thoughts and actions my character would be engaged in during the firefight. No one may realize it from the credits, but he was an integral part of my performance.

A quick aside about transformation is a story from the hair and makeup trailer on *Wind River*. While applying the scratch marks to my face that related to the storyline, the makeup artist said that I looked familiar. I had been working on *Scandal* at the time as well, where I played the sex worker who was engaged in a same-sex relationship, and when I mentioned the show she said she was a huge fan of it and had seen every episode. Without revealing my character, I merely said, "Oh, then you'd know me." I told her I was going to let her figure it out on her own and she seemed stumped. The next day, in the middle of applying the scratch marks again, she said, "Oh my God! You play Michael!" Here I was, talking with her face to face; she had seen me in a multitude of episodes of a show where I was not using an accent and looked relatively the same as I did on this movie. But the support of the projects and the context of two very different stories had produced a transformation in her perception of me.

Another example of transformation came from the help I received from the hair and makeup departments on Amazon's *Goliath*. My character, Danny Loomis, undergoes his own transformation throughout the second season. When we first meet him, he is the alpha dog in his relationship with his friend Keith Roman, whom he is using for his own benefit. He is clean-cut and confident. By the end of the season, after we've seen him physically beaten by his billionaire boss and feeling the squeeze of an even more powerful evil nemesis, he has become unraveled. Nina Paskowitz and Geri Oppenheim, the hair and makeup heads, helped the visuals of this transformation immensely. We joked about my facial hair needing a separate credit for it's "performance" on the show. Joking aside, their attention to the detail of where my character was in his journey in any given scene added to the overall magic of his demise. Most viewers may not notice that kind of detail, but I know that my performance would have been significantly diminished without their help.

There is generally a lack of fanfare around those who *aid* the prime transformer because when their work is well-done, it does not call attention to itself. As legendary director Sidney Lumet mentions in his incredible book, *Making Movies*, if the transformation is pulled off the way it's supposed to be, viewers will sometimes complain that nothing happened. One particularly famous story involves Lumet's film adaptation of Eugene O'Neill's stage play *Long Day's Journey into Night*. Lumet and cinematographer Boris Kaufman went to great lengths to visually aid the actors' transformations from early in the film to their climactic finish. Their techniques included very specific lighting and framing choices for each character that progressed as the film continued. Ultimately, many critics said that Lumet had merely "filmed the play," which only proves the subtlety of the filmmakers' visual strategies and the success of the magic trick they pulled off.

There are many times, as an actor, where the preparation that I do for a role is mostly for *me*. In 2015 I did a pilot for a period show that took place in 1947 Hollywood. I was playing the heavy, the muscle behind the studio head. In the pilot, I had to knock one guy out with a punch and beat up a spoiled movie star in a back alley. The way the scenes were being shot, it would have been easy to rely on the camera work and editing to tell the story. But, for my own ability to believe myself in this role, I hired ex-Olympian turned boxing coach José Navarro to help me with my foot work. Because the pilot was being shot so quickly after I got the job, we only had time for a few sessions beforehand, so I did the best I could. But I wanted to know what it felt like in my body to move like a fighter and think like a fighter, so after shooting the pilot I hired him and trained with him for months while eagerly anticipating the news of our show being picked up. No one else may have ever noticed the difference, but this training was more for me, to help me believe in my own ability to pull off the transformation. Ultimately, the pilot never went to series, so the results of my training were never seen. But that doesn't take away from the lessons I learned from the talented people I had the great fortune to work with.

Transformation begins with the belief that we can in fact transform. While there are as many techniques out there as there are teachers, the most important aspects of it are that it is possible and it is best approached by keeping in mind that for a true transformation to take place, time is needed. With patience, intention, hard work, and a team of supporters and mentors, you can change more than you realize if it is what you truly desire. Quick fixes may get you there temporarily, but as you've heard from others who have done it, lasting change requires lasting changes of habits and routines.

Top Three Takeaways

1. The fact that nature is full of examples of extreme transformation should inspire us to believe we are capable of it, too.

2. Don Saladino's magic transformation tip: Do less, not more, in the beginning. Small changes yield larger transformation in the long run.

3. Don't think you need to do it all on your own. Behind every great transformation is a large team. Learn from them and be grateful for them.

CHAPTER

10

Leadership

"It all starts with humility. Everything I've learned about leadership, whether it's fatherhood, being a husband, being a fullback ... if you're not humble, you don't have a chance to be happy in this life."

—Heath Evans, 10-Year NFL Veteran,
Super Bowl Champion

One of the benefits of sitting down on my *10,000 NOs* podcast with so many guests who have made larger-than-average impacts by leading men and women through various organizations and teams is that I've been able to boil down their intricate stories and varied backgrounds into simple-to-digest commonalities. Each episode, just like each chapter in this book, concludes with Three Takeaways. Regardless of the various words, phrases, and metaphors that different people from different industries, cultures, and walks of life use, I have found three overall tenets on great leadership that apply to all of them: *service*, *communication*, and *accountability*.

You Can't Have *Leader*ship Without *Relationships*

Service, in this context, pertains to the leader basing each and every one of their actions, as well as every command or assignment given to their team, on a mandate to *serve the higher good* of the organization's mission statement. This means that team members will only be asked to carry out tasks that serve the organization's stated purpose, rather than orders that solely benefit the leader.

Communication is the leader's ability to *convey* the mission statement to team members clearly and concisely and to work with teammates to come up with *actionable* tasks to achieve the overall philosophy of the organization.

Accountability is the leader's obligation to take total *responsibility* for both the good *and the bad* that happens on their watch. While the leader usually receives the lion's share of praise and financial reward when things go right, they must also be willing to accept responsibility and blame when things go wrong, even if the mistakes and missteps were the fault of someone other than themselves. These truisms hold up in business, sports, and the entertainment industry, as well as in our homes every day.

Don't Be a Grinch: Serve

When I was a teenager, my friend and I had summer jobs at an iron mill. We learned many lessons about being good workers that summer by being put in charge of menial tasks that could have been done by monkeys. My biggest takeaway, however, was something the foreman, Robbie, shared with us one day. Robbie was a great leader, respected by everyone who worked for him, including guys twice his size and covered in tattoos. When we asked him how he did it, his answer was simple, "I'm willing to do everything I ask my men to do. Usually they can do their specific task better than me, but they've seen me jump in the trenches and dig when it needed to be done." It was his willingness to get his hands dirty that helped his employees to know that they were *contributing* to Robbie's cause, but not being exploited by him while doing so. His willingness to get dirty was *not* an attempt to be liked. People did end up liking him, but his motivation was more pure than that: he was placing the needs of the company above his personal need to be comfortable and stay clean.

Even superstars know the importance of putting the good of the team in front of their own personal goals. Before Boston College Women's Lacrosse Coach Acacia Walker was considered the elite of college coaches, she was one of the best players in the world. In 1999, at age 15, Walker was the youngest member of the world championship Under-19 US team that won gold in Perth, Australia; she won another gold medal in the 2009 World Cup, playing on the US Women's Senior National Lacrosse team in Prague, Czech Republic. She was an All-American player as an undergrad at the University of Maryland and Assistant Coach at Northwestern when they won three consecutive NCAA National Championships. Her individual statistics notwithstanding, when Walker spoke to me for *10,000 NOs* it was clear she held one virtue much higher than anything else: serve your team.

> "You give up everything about your own self and then you turn around and you have everything that you'll ever need."
>
> —*Acacia Walker, Head Coach,*
> *Boston College Women's Lacrosse*

Service

I mentioned Sharran Srivatsaa's "10Xing" of Teles Properties' annual revenue in Chapter 4. Shrivatsaa has a background as a financial analyst at Goldman Sachs, and before that, he was a competitive tennis player. This combination led him to bring two unique beliefs to Teles: (1) Numbers don't lie; and (2) With a strong mental game you can overcome opponents more naturally gifted than you. Using very simple, pragmatic questions, he got the company onboard with what seemed at the time like an impossible task: to be valued high enough to be sold at a profit before the beginning of the next natural real estate cycle that would make the partners' efforts worthwhile.

While this may sound like it is above the average person's mathematical and financial capabilities, the *execution* of Shrivatsaa's strategy came down to a simple plan and incredible leadership. Once they settled on the number they needed to hit to reach their goal ($3 billion in annual revenue), they put systems into place that would help them reach it. Literally every single decision the company made from that point forward was vetted to make sure that it was in *service* to that number being hit, forcing them to think big.

As stated earlier, this mandate was *communicated* with the utmost care and detail through annual, monthly, weekly, and daily meetings in which every employee was drilled repeatedly with the company's overarching goal in relation to even the smallest tasks. Shrivatsaa, as the leader, was willing to take full *accountability* if the plan he developed caused the company to implode, even while knowing that the chances of pulling it off were extremely risky in the highly competitive world of commercial real estate.

Luckily for Shrivatsaa, the plan worked. Countless companies and business leaders today seek him out to bestow his wisdom upon them and their organizations. I have personally seen him speak on four occasions, and each time he reinvents his material. He is a reminder that reaching the upper echelons of business leadership is not unlike being an elite player in the NBA or in any other field: despite the incredibly long hours he has put into preparing, the end result is so natural and graceful that it appears he is just making it up on the spot.

Communication

In the last chapter, I referenced director Sidney Lumet's book, *Making Movies*, to illustrate a point about transformation. But really, that book, which is full of examples of his filmmaking process, is a proverbial symposium on great leadership. Perhaps Lumet's prime tool in leadership is his communication style. Throughout his career directing films, he took great effort and time to make sure that his vision of the script's underlying theme and essence was understood by each and every department head. Long conversations, in which he would sit down with these department heads months in advance of production to hone the ways in which they could execute within their area of responsibility, stressed an understanding of one another's visions. From his initial production meetings, through the chaos of the shoot, and all the way into the editing rooms of post-production, he wanted everyone on the same page. Tellingly, he ends each chapter of his book with the phrase, "We were all making the same movie."

One of my most rewarding experiences as an actor came under the guidance of showrunner and director Lawrence Trilling, who, when directing, operates in the same vein as Lumet. On one of my first days on set for *Goliath*, I told Trilling I had an idea I wanted to try as I entered the scene, which took place on a basketball court. He said, "Show me. If I need to pull you back, I will." While this may sound like a lack of direction and communication, for me it was the opposite. The message I received was: *I trust you. That's why I hired you. I want your ideas, but I am also here to guide you if those ideas take us away from my overall vision.* When I reminded him of this moment during our conversation on *10,000 NOs*, Trilling explained that his openness in his directing style was not a reflection of him being *nice*.

> "I do have an ego. I care about doing great work and I want the great work to reflect well on me, like anybody. I'm definitely in the 'Best Idea Wins' business, but I also like to be the one who is the filter through which the ideas pass, so that's ego, too. I still get to decide."
>
> —*Lawrence Trilling, Director/Producer*

Much like Lumet, Trilling was not only this way with his actors. The hair and makeup department heads on *Goliath* drastically improved my performance with their contributions to it. When I remarked how specific they were and how much they helped me, they credited Trilling's directing style. They said he was one of their favorite directors when it came to collaboration because his trust in them was matched by his ability to explain exactly what he needed in any given circumstance. But his specificity did not handcuff them. He didn't tell them *how* to do their job. Instead, he trusted that when he told them *what* he needed, they would use their unique talents and skills to deliver it in a way that was far better than he could have imagined himself.

Accountability

Whether it is the most powerful star on a set or a well-known director, when a movie strikes a chord with audiences and becomes a box office smash, the person with the largest reputation or most power is generally perceived as the hero. And when a movie bombs at the box office, that same person is usually the one who ends up vilified and blamed for the failure. True leaders take both the good and the bad with dignity. In doing so, they gain the respect of their followers, employees, teammates, or family members.

> "When you're sitting on the doctor's examining table with wires hanging off you, being tested for signs of a heart attack, none of that matters. Bad partners, lazy employees, and needy clients didn't land me in front of a doctor—I did. It was *my* fault."
>
> —*Bedros Keuilian, Author,* Man Up

When I helped Chris Messina behind the scenes on his directorial debut, *Alex of Venice*, I was privy to the sage advice his wife, Jennifer Todd, gave him. Todd is a prolific producer, and also a guest of *10,000 NOs* podcast, who is considered among the elite in Hollywood. She knew that Messina would be extremely prepared and know what he wanted, but she advised him to be open to great ideas regardless of where they came from. She said that, in working with first-time directors, she had observed some of them fail to take great ideas from someone with a less prestigious title on set for fear of appearing weak in front of cast and crew. They did not know what Todd knew, that there is a system of accountability that could not be avoided on a film. She explained, "Take great ideas, even if they come from a production assistant (a low-status position on a set), because by the time the film comes out, it's the director who will get the credit. But don't feel bad about that because, if the film fails, you'll take *all the blame* for every one of those ideas, too."

Humility: Next-Level Leadership

While humility is tied to service, it is worth pointing out that some leaders use the above three tenets and then transcend even other top leaders by exhibiting ample amounts of humility. It is difficult for me to have a chapter on leadership and not include a short story about my friend Chris Burns. I've written about Burns in these pages earlier; he has not just been elite in one field, but two: as a US Navy SEAL and now a trauma surgeon. He came to visit me and my family in Los Angeles last year on his way to a medical convention. After a run on the beach, we sat in the sand and reminisced about the past. As we sifted through our greatest hits, laughing and also hitting some deeper topics, I made a nonchalant remark about my college lacrosse coach. "I can't believe Moy cut you. I mean, you were a Navy SEAL for God's sake! How could you not have made that team? You were certainly a better athlete than I was." Burns looked at me, not sure if he should divulge a secret he'd been keeping for almost 30 years.

Finally, he said, "You know, I actually didn't get cut. Coach told me I had made the team, but I had to let him know that I'd miss a lot of practices and even some games because of my ROTC commitment." He had to make a choice and his Navy scholarship took precedent over playing lacrosse. But at the time, when some of our other friends who hadn't made the team announced to the rest of us that they and Burns had been cut, he chose not to shame them by explaining what had really happened with him. Instead, he remained silent.

For 30 years, he allowed all of us to think he had been cut for lack of ability even though that wasn't the case. Reflecting on that story, it is not shocking to see how the rest of his life has played out since then. A true leader, like Burns, inspires others to act honorably and with humility. Our world might be in better shape if there were more leaders like that and fewer that fall back on chest-thumping and making others feel worse about themselves.

Delegating: The Art of Getting Help

In my career, my awareness of my own potential to lead eluded me for a long time. In keeping with the idea of accountability I described at the beginning of this chapter, I knew there was no one to blame more than me for my career being in a place where I felt compelled to start a podcast called *10,000 NOs* at age 45 rather than collecting Oscars and Emmy Awards. I was finally brought to the point where I was forced to confront my own shortcomings and how they contributed to the wide gap I saw between where I *wanted* my career to be and where it actually resided. What I learned was that possibly the biggest culprit in my not being where I wanted to be was my lack of *self-leadership*. Specifically, it was in how I related to my representatives. While I had heard the overused adage that "you don't work for your agents, they work for you" many times over, I was not fully *acting* on it. It was not until I felt the financial crunch on my family that resulted from my lack of leadership that I got serious and specific about how I wanted my representatives to help my cause.

> "Then I started realizing, and this is no fault to the people I was working with, they had their jobs ... My job was to be the visionary, to see around the corner. And I had a vision in my head, of the show, that they didn't know because maybe I wasn't clear with them."
> —*Steven Kane, Creator/Director/Producer,*
> The Last Ship

My relationship with my managers and agents has always been good on a personal level, but as a business owner and operator, which is how I've come to see myself in show business in addition to being an artist, I was leaving way too much up to chance. I wasn't using the aforementioned tenets of leadership to squeeze the most out of these incredible resources, who had relationships with so many people who could employ me because they interacted with them through their other clients' business affairs. I was too passive when it came to our interactions. Ironically for an actor known to be a "talker" by his family and friends, as well as a good listener, my biggest failure was in the communication portion of leadership. I knew what I wanted and I was willing to give blood in service of it. I was also willing to take the blame when things didn't turn out the way I wished they would. But I was not communicating my desires clearly enough.

Part of my lack of communication with my representatives stemmed from a lack of clarity as to what I wanted specifically and a desire to be liked and not "rock the boat." I'll dive into those more later, but for now, part of my failure in this area came from my mistakenly assuming that my reps would be bothered if, for example, they hustled to get me an audition only to have me pass on it. Luckily, my tight friendship with Chris Messina, who handles this aspect of his career better than most, gave me insight on what I was failing to do. When I finally took my reps out to lunch to explain exactly what I needed and what I was willing to do and *not* do to reach my goals, they were beyond excited. In retrospect, the idea that they would be bothered by my desire to pass on smaller jobs in pursuit of larger ones is insane. They make their living off of percentages of the incomes of the artists they represent, so the better I do, the better they do. That said, our new mission statement, while exciting, also brought about many new challenges and opportunities for more leadership.

Much like the hysterical yet anxiety-inducing opening to *Jerry Maguire*, where one late night Jerry drafts a mission statement to his entire company urging them to care less about money and more about compassion and personal relationships, the excitement of my new mandate to my representatives quickly translated into a massive slowdown in activity. By choosing to give out some of my own "no"s to my pile of 10,000, I was choosing to have significantly fewer opportunities. This created many situations where my team and I were confronted with the choice of giving in to the need of immediate financial relief, by going in for smaller gigs that were not very artistically or financially rewarding, or passing and holding out for gigs more aligned with our highest view of my career. With very few exceptions in dire situations, we remained true to our vision and it shifted my career drastically in the direction I was looking to take it.

> "You can lose your Twitter account. You can lose your website, you can lose your email list, but if you have your relationships, you're gonna be just fine even though you don't necessarily believe it."
> —*Jordan Harbinger, Top Podcaster/Speaker,*
> The Art of Charm, The Jordan Harbinger Show

While my lunch with my representatives predated the launch of *10,000 NOs*, it is no coincidence that my career's most dramatic progress has overlapped with all of the conversations I have been lucky enough to have as a result of the podcast. Coming face to face with people who have done the things I had read about for years in business and self-development books proved to contain the leadership lessons that I needed. When things felt overwhelming or impossible, I could draw on a story told to me by Alison Levine, who willingly put her life on the line to climb Mount Everest and the highest peaks on all seven continents despite being born with a hole in her heart. Likewise, cancer survivors like Elissa Goodman and Paige Davis, or Rob Whitaker, who lost his battle with cancer after our conversation, have taught me that courageous decisions that come along with leadership have to be made even under—especially under—the worst of circumstances.

While the circumstances of a grueling season of television cannot really compare to those of cancer survivors or mountain climbers, they do provide a glimpse into the effects of a great leader's ability to make a work environment welcoming and productive. Conversely, they can show us how a terrible leader can make a workplace intolerable. While I will not name names exemplifying the latter, I have worked on sets that were miserable because the person with the most power set a poor example of complaining, phoning in their performance, treating others on the cast and crew with no respect, and being more interested in going home than actually doing the work for which they were being paid exorbitant amounts of money. Luckily, though, I have been very fortunate to have worked with some great actors who also happen to be great human beings. Those great leaders motivate everyone around them to strive and treat everyone around them with dignity.

On film and TV productions, a call sheet contains all of the information every cast and crew member needs to know for the following day's work. It includes the location, the scenes that need to be shot, and each member of the cast and crew required to be present, as well as the time they need to show up to work (call time). Each cast member is assigned a number, by which they are identified throughout the production, to simplify the instructions from the producers and shield them from having to write out the full name of every actor working in each scene. The actor who is listed as number one on the call sheet, the lead role on a film or TV show, is generally the person who sets the tone on a production, particularly in television, where the directors are often guests invited to direct an episode or two and then be on their way. Producers and showrunners are obviously huge forces as well, but the actor is more visible and thus, usually more influential to the vibe of a set.

Fans of *Scandal* often ask me what it was like to work on that set. I always respond that I have never seen a group of actors collectively more excited and grateful for their jobs than I saw on that set. They clapped and cheered for every guest actor who was announced at their weekly table reads. I never heard any complaints about the long hours. People were genuinely excited to be there, even after shooting over one hundred episodes. While Shonda Rhimes deserves the credit for assembling such a nice group of team players, Kerry Washington's temperament is what set the tone. She was always prepared, engaged, kind to those around her, and welcoming. There was an ease and grace that let everyone on set know that this was the way in which we treat people, and our work, around here.

Big Star Does Not Mean Oversized Ego

The first day I worked with Jimmy Smits on *The West Wing*, I remember our van ride back to our trailers. As a sign of respect, the biggest star is generally assumed to take the shotgun position, giving them the most space. Smits, who was far higher on the call sheet than any of the rest of us who were packed into the van, had jammed his six-foot, four-inch frame into the back row, making room for others to pile in. When the van stopped at his trailer first to drop him off, rather than make everyone move, he said, "I'm fine" and proceeded to climb over the back seat and hop out of the rear of the van. I instantly loved the guy for his humility. What I admired even more as I got to know him over the following year, working long hours with him, was that this persona was not some publicity stunt to make him appear to be a man of the people. That was just his essence. Smits did not sacrifice his work in order to be liked. James Gandolfini had a similar approach on *The Sopranos*: when it came time to work there was a laser focus. Both were good, kind men who were very generous and helpful to me as a young actor. But they were not being nice to me to win my favor. They were leaders, inspiring me to approach my work with as much intensity as they did. They also treated everyone on the cast and crew with as much respect as they showed each director. In my opinion, their leadership and humility is at least partially responsible for the success of those shows.

I have examples of the generosity of stars I've worked with that could fill another book. The point of bringing up these stories is the context of *when* these individuals displayed such virtue. Television and film shoots can stretch out for a long time. While the challenge can be the acting, I think more of the challenge is being camera ready, knowing that millions of people will eventually be able to see one's face through eternity. Actors have to be camera ready even at 3 a.m. at the end of a long week of shooting, when Friday night has become Saturday morning, affectionately known in the business as Fraturday. These leaders exhibited that kind of discipline and respect even when they were frazzled and exhausted. Yes, Reese Witherspoon impressed me when she went around the table and shook hands, introducing herself to every single person present at our first table read for *Hot Pursuit*. But what endeared her to me even more is when, months after we wrapped, I was walking down a Los Angeles sidewalk when an SUV with tinted windows whizzed past me. Witherspoon's head popped out and she yelled, "Matt!" She didn't have to do that, but it made me feel valued. That's just one of the leadership qualities that points to why she makes millions of dollars and is beloved by so many. She recognizes that relationships are what is important and they don't end, or have to end, just because we've finished shooting. She is a leader.

Leaders come in all shapes, sizes, and styles. Some may be boisterous, intensely getting in your face and screaming, while others are quiet, pulling their teammates aside to give them gentle counsel. Either way, the best leaders serve a common goal, whether it is to make the best film, be the best team, or build the best company. Practicing what they preach is a prerequisite for great leaders, as anyone with children knows: they will do what you *do*, not what you *say*. Wherever you are on the spectrum of leadership, you can increase your skills by being decisive yet respectful and bold yet humble.

Top Three Takeaways

1. The primary aspect of leadership is service to the greater good.
2. The best way to learn how to be a great leader is to surround yourself with great leaders and learn from their ways.
3. Lead by example. People will do what you *do*, not what you *say*.

CHAPTER

11

Meditation and Relaxation

"I just love it. It's like a washing machine for your brain. It's beautiful. It's graceful. It's exciting. It's delicious. It's one of the great sounds of all time to *be*, and to hear that water rush by you, either in a boat or standing in it."
—Henry Winkler, Emmy Award–Winning Actor,
on the meditative qualities of fly fishing

My college roommates and I, having seen *Caddyshack* more times than we care to admit, have been quoting Chevy Chase's character since our freshman year: "Be the ball, Danny." In the context of this hilarious comedy, the line induces laughter. It's delivered a little tongue-in-cheek, and yet it is also the underlying theme to the entire film. Danny Noonan, who works as a caddy to Chase's Ty Webb, carrying his bags around the course for some pocket cash, really wants to be a pro golfer himself.

While the movie is full of quotable lines and amazingly funny sequences, it has held up over time because underneath all the laughs is a meditative message about letting go of the pressures society has placed upon you and allowing yourself the space and relaxation to fully take advantage of the gifts you have at your disposal.

Welcome to the New Age

The trends have changed immensely since *Caddyshack* debuted in 1980, particularly society's view of eastern philosophies and practices. While I can't recall any pro athletes pointing to meditation as part of their training regimen when I was a kid, today I can point to Steph Curry's 2017 commercial for Kaiser Permanente in which he lays in a float tank, visualizing himself performing all kinds of feats with a basketball. Or superstar quarterback Tom Brady's TB12 method, which stresses practices like stretching, deep-tissue massage, and abstinence from sugar, alcohol, and caffeine, as well as ample of amounts of hydration and sleep. While such practices had a reputation of being "unmanly" back when I was a kid, they have rapidly shifted into the consciousness of the mainstream in recent years. The reason for this shift is simple: meditation and relaxation produce results that cannot be denied.

> "I was just as skeptical as you and I came to this so reluctantly. I literally had miraculous results with my daughter when she was very, very sick. She had an immunological condition."
>
> —*Amy Budden, Meditation Teacher and Certified Hypnotherapist*

If you are shifting uncomfortably in your chair as you read this, you are not alone. My own relationship to meditation and relaxation, if visually charted on a graph, would resemble that of a rollercoaster ride. Being a product of a traditional East Coast upbringing, surrounded by many people who have gone on to successful careers in industries that could be described as more tangible than mine, I was resistant to meditation when first introduced to it. Only in looking back do I realize I was studying and practicing aspects of meditation long before I had a term to apply to it. Acting, in many ways, borrows so many principles from meditation. Without realizing it, I already was utilizing certain techniques that are very much in line with what I have since been exposed to through meditation practitioners I have interviewed and befriended. And yet, when I first attempted to meditate in the traditional sense, I had one recurring thought: "This is not for me."

Because of this rocky relationship, I feel qualified to serve as a bridge between meditation proponents and those who have never dabbled in, or can't envision themselves ever benefiting from, meditation. If, on the other hand, you happen to have a firm meditation practice in place, feel free to skip ahead.

Take me with a grain of salt, and please refrain from judging me if you're a traditionalist, but I believe there are many ways to meditate that do not involve sitting in a pretzel-like position on a yoga mat. In fact, a more relaxed interpretation of the art espoused by the popular app Headspace is what got me meditating in the first place. Full disclosure: as of this writing, I have not used Headspace for any significant amount of time and I do not engage regularly in what I would call a meditation practice. However, I do employ a bastardized and personalized version of meditation every day of my life. In many respects, that's the point of meditation: practicing it in a way that works best for you.

While there is a part of me that is ashamed to admit that I don't spend an hour every morning and evening meditating, I feel that admitting it to you is actually part of my meditative practice. This is because, at least in my simple understanding of the art, at its core meditation is about accepting things *as they are*, not *as we wish them to be*. So if we have a thought that could be labeled as "not good," rather than judge it and lacerate ourselves for having that thought, meditation encourages us to breathe and release it. The image that made sense for me was to imagine my thoughts as constantly floating down a river, each like a small boat. Just because they float by, we are not required to jump on each and every one. In fact, it's probably a good idea *not* to jump on the ones that will likely send us over a waterfall. In the same way, rather than hiding my lack of practice from you and presenting myself as someone who "has it all," as I'd love to see myself, I am choosing to show you the way I *really am*. The truth is that, while I may someday engage in a more rigorous daily meditation practice, right now I do not. And that's okay. We can just chalk it up as another of my 10,000 "no"s. And wherever you happen to be in your practice right now is also okay. But maybe in learning more about this, you will add it to your ever-growing evolution toward becoming your best self.

Being a Straight-A Student Is Overrated

One of my first acting teachers in New York City was Terry Schreiber. I studied with him for four years and learned many things about the craft of acting, and myself, at his T. Schreiber Studio. Terry introduced me to a warm-up exercise that is rooted in the same fundamentals as meditation: breath work. Terry also encouraged me to look at myself in a way that was different than I had up until that point. My *real* education from Terry, however, came via something he said to me repeatedly that backed up the principles of meditation that were practiced in those breathing exercises. Terry's recurring statement, to me specifically, in that scene-study class was, "Don't try to be such a straight-A student."

Something I've come to know, after seeing and assessing many performances over the years, is that bad acting can often be traced back to an actor attempting to present themself as *having it all figured out*. When I catch glimpses of it in my own performances, causing me to cringe, I remember why Terry worked so hard to break me of the habit. What he was doing, while it wasn't called by this name, had its roots in meditation. It started with the physicality and relaxation that was trained in the exercise I'm about to describe, so I'll begin with that and work my way forward from there so you can see the link. You can then choose to apply some or all of the principles to your own life.

Grounding Exercise

1. Standing up, with feet pointed forward and barely touching one another, interlock your hands by intertwining your fingers the way that comes naturally to you.

2. Shift your interlocked fingers so that they are interlocked the opposite way (whichever hand was dominant is now shifted and reversed; this sends a message to your brain that helps get you out of your habitual patterns).

3. Turn your interlocked palms toward the floor and bend your knees slightly. Be mindful of tension that may be present in your neck and shoulders by bringing awareness to that area and breathing into the tension to release it.

4. Keep your upper body straight, not through a rigid attempt to stay straight but by imagining a string that

extends from your pelvis up through your torso and out the top of your head. Begin to bob up and down slightly, bending at the knees and hips.

5. While doing this, imagine three points on the bottom of each of your feet (at the heel, the ball of your foot, and the outside of your foot across from the ball) growing roots that break down through the floorboards or earth below you and sink deep down under the surface, grounding you.

6. As you move gently and rhythmically up and down, inhale and exhale through your nose with gentle bursts of air that release at the bottom of each bob.

7. Throughout this exercise, be mindful of tension in your sphincter and release it. (While this last instruction usually brought awkward giggles from young jackasses like myself back then, it has proven to be very useful throughout my career.) Be mindful of tension everywhere, particularly in your calves, and shift your center of gravity in a way that relieves you as much of that tension as possible.

8. Many times the bobbing will cause a burning sensation in the thighs as they are doing most of the work. Breathe into the burning sensation and do your best to accept it. After a period of time, usually when the burning feels like it's too much for you to handle, gently slow down the bouncing to a stop, with your knees bent.

9. Working to overcome the pain of the burn, stay relaxed and bent, which keeps pressure on those thighs. Keep your knees together, and swish your hips side to side, as if you are a duck waddling its tail.

10. After about ten swishes in total, come to a rest again. Your thighs will definitely be burning by now, but you're not done. Remaining in position, you will now bend your knees and hips even more, lowering yourself by a few inches, into a slightly deeper bend.

11. Begin again with steps 4 through 10. Particularly focus on the relaxation aspects amid the fatigue of your thighs, and envision the roots extending from your feet sinking into the ground. This is where I get the most reward from this exercise. When you've reached your threshold, slowly bring the bounce to a stop and extend your legs straight, standing up. You can unclasp your hands from each other and shake out any tension.

The end result, if you do this even for only two minutes, is that you will feel much more grounded in your body. It is as if you've been in a self-induced trance. Blood circulates throughout your extremities. I have employed this exercise for decades now, before auditions, in my trailer when shooting, or whenever I have felt the need to be more grounded. It can be used before a big presentation, a job interview, or just when you wake up in the morning to start your day. It gifts you with being in touch with your physicality and less in your own head.

Hopefully you can see that one of the lessons of this exercise is linked directly to the image I presented earlier about not attaching ourselves to every thought that passes by as it floats down the river. In this instance, the burning in the thighs is no longer in control of shutting us down. We can acknowledge it, but also let it pass by while we instead focus on our breath, relaxation, and grounding. It is an exercise in accepting what is and carrying on regardless.

Much in the same way, Terry's advice, "Don't try to be such a straight-A student," was his way of telling me to accept my whole self. What he noticed in my work was that I was only revealing the aspects of myself that were strong and smart and "together." He explained, "We don't come to the theater to see that. We want to see what's *underneath*. What are you struggling with? What's complicated? What's unresolved? We want to see you work that out right in front of our eyes. Don't hide behind this persona you've created of this guy that has it all. That's not very interesting. And, more importantly, it's not truthful."

"You Are Enough"

Another acting coach, Kim Gillingham, whom I mentioned in an earlier chapter, had her mantra, "You are enough." She would often say that the root of bad acting is an actor feeling that they are not enough on their own, which prompts them to overcompensate and give a false and overdone performance. These principles may apply to acting, but they also apply to anything and everything. Every entrepreneur I've sat down with on *10,000 NOs* has stressed that, underneath all of the various systems they may come up with to run their business, there is a simplicity to their success: find something that people need help with, and figure out a solution. That requires really looking at a situation *as it is*: the good, the bad, and the ugly. Each cancer survivor, and other guests of mine who have suffered some kind of trauma, has expressed the same sentiment: *it was only when I finally accepted my new circumstances as they were, that I was able to start moving forward again.*

"You don't need Stage IV cancer … everybody's got somewhere on that scale, right? And if you think you're at the worst end of your scale? That feels the same as the worst end of my scale, so it's never a comparison of, 'Ew, my tragedy beats your tragedy.'"

—*Rob Whitaker, on his fight with Stage IV colon cancer*

All of this covers the acceptance portion of meditation, but there is a whole treasure chest of tools available to us, which I have yet to fully access but hope to over time. This is the reason meditation has grown so much in popularity in recent years; just as my entrepreneurial friends stated their need to serve people in order for their company's services to be valued, meditation has increasingly served more people, particularly in the area of performance. While Western civilization used to, and in many cases still does, have a bias against Eastern philosophies as being "woo-woo" and "touchy feely," more recent studies, such as the one by Sara Lazar, a neuroscientist at Mass General Hospital and Harvard Medical School, have unearthed the science behind meditation and relaxation. Brain scans of control groups revealed that meditation practice has the ability to *physically* alter the grooves in our brain, thus altering our experience of the world and our ability to succeed. According to Brigid Shulte in "Harvard Neuroscientist: Meditation Not Only Reduces Stress, Here's How It Changes Your Brain" in the *Washington Post* (May 26, 2015), Lazar's study found that, "Long term meditators were revealed to have an increased amount of gray matter in the insula and sensory regions, the auditory and sensory cortex. They also found they had more gray matter in the frontal cortex, which is associated with working memory and executive decision making."

"Sara Lazar is a Harvard neurologist. She did before-
and-afters of the brains of people who had never
meditated, fifty years old and up, to people who had
meditated nonstop for twenty-three minutes a day for
eight weeks and their brains changed."
                          —*Suze Yalof Schwartz, Founder/CEO,*
                                          Unplug Meditation

In the 1970s, Richard Bandler and John Grinder studied
brain chemistry and the effects of language and behavior on the
brain. With their 1979 book *Frogs into Princes*, they began what
was eventually known as NLP, neuro-linguistic programming.
When it first emerged, many leaders in the medical field in the
United States laughed it off as being practiced by kooks on the
fringes of society. But results have a way of silencing critics and
making their way to center stage when they are undeniable, and
that's what has happened with NLP.

"I meditate every day. I do it in the mornings for about
10 to 15 minutes. I think it's important because it sets
me up for the rest of the day."
                          —*Kobe Bryant, NBA Superstar*

That Kobe Bryant meditated may not seem surprising to
you if you're under the age of 30 and grew up with athletes
speaking this way about meditation. In my childhood these trains
of thought could not have been further away from how the best
athletes generally looked at self-knowledge, or at philosophies
with even remote ties to what was considered the more "femi-
nine" side of our nature. More typically, male athletic prowess
was presented in a way best summed up by NFL superstar

Jack Lambert: "I believe the game is designed to reward the ones who hit the hardest … if you can't take it, you shouldn't play!"

In fact, it was only in writing this book that my own memory was jogged about a book I read in junior high that had a profound effect, though I had long since forgotten about it. It was all-star basketball player Kareem Abdul-Jabbar's autobiography, *Giant Steps*. Looking back, I now remember that his story, and the way he framed it, resonated with me as I was going through puberty. He writes of feeling like an outsider who was trapped in his own head, a victim to his thoughts and intellect. But he found salvation, and incredible results, through his study of martial arts. The same principles of meditation and relaxation discussed here were then an integral part of what he took with him from his martial arts practice and translated into his prolific career on the basketball court.

> "I can do something else besides stuff a ball through a hoop. My biggest resource is my mind."
>
> *Kareem Abdul-Jabbar, NBA Superstar*

I wish I could present myself as the guy who is levitating at his keyboard while writing this, but that would not be true. Besides, I believe you'll learn more from my failures than successes, so I'd like to revisit a story I first covered in the chapter on risk. The way I presented the period following my stint on *The Sopranos*, when I convinced my new bride to quit her job and follow me west for pilot season, it may have sounded like I was the victim of terrible luck as I rifled through wedding money and returned to New York forced to bartend once again. But let's assess that trip through a different lens.

At the end of 2002, I was coming off my biggest successes up until that time, both professionally and personally. Success can feed the ego, even if we are cognizant of this tendency, as I believed I was at the time. If I could go back to 2003 and interview 30-year-old Matt Del Negro, I would have found him to be humble and hardworking. However, if I were to *really* look at him closely, I would have discovered he was scared, anxious, and possibly too ambitious for his own good. Success, in the traditional sense, implies some kind of external validation. Both being part of a hit show and marrying a kind, beautiful woman are an excess of external validation. Without realizing it, I was being set up for a fall because my appetite had been whetted by the success I had attained, and I wanted more. *Results* became more important to me in that period of time than *process*. That is a dangerous way to live and, in retrospect, I now realize that meditation and relaxation would have served me immensely through that period.

I believe it was mostly fear that drove me. I felt like the iron was hot and I needed to strike. Auditions and meetings were flying at me at a much more rapid pace than I had previously experienced. And the mood toward me, and my value as an actor, was noticeably more receptive than ever because I was now associated with a well-respected show. This combination created a frenzy mindset that was the opposite of meditative. While I don't fault myself for mistakenly relying on my *grind* rather than my *flow*, I see now the error of my ways.

Had I used the Special Forces mantra I recently learned of—"Slow is smooth and smooth is fast"—and taken the slower, smoother route in 2003, perhaps I would have had more success that spring. If you're thinking I'm being too self-critical and it was just a matter of bad luck and unfortunate timing, you could be right. But that interpretation renders me powerless by forcing me to think of myself as a defenseless victim who is at the mercy of the whims of the universe.

While we are susceptible to the forces that bang up against us, we are also capable of incorporating practices that aid our chances of success. In this case, examining my actions and acknowledging where I could have made different choices without judging myself or going against my character, I can use the principles of meditation to let some of those previous habits and choices flow down the river so I can choose new ones the next time I'm in a similar situation.

> "If I kept busy, if I kept myself in perpetual motion, I wouldn't have to answer, I wouldn't have to look into my soul. And so the universe gave me about three warnings. And, in the end, went, 'Oh, okay, girl. You are gonna be slapped down and slapped down hard and now you have to face it and now you have to deal with it.'"
> —*Sue Hollis, Named One of Australia's Top 10 Female Entrepreneurs by* SmartCompany

The simultaneous beauty and curse of meditative practices is that we never graduate from them. Even the most enlightened individuals are engaged in consciously detaching themselves from results for the rest of their lives. So maybe the next time you do attempt to pull out a yoga mat and follow a meditation app, an actual teacher, or your own breath, you will go easier on yourself and accept wherever it is that you are in that moment. From experience, this is not easy to do, but it is a necessary part of anyone's journey toward success in any field, as well as anyone's fulfillment in this life. Believe it or not, sometimes stopping to smell the roses will get you to your destination faster than sprinting as fast as you can, ignoring what's around you.

Top Three Takeaways

1. Meditation has grown in popularity because it has produced great results. It is worth trying if you have not yet done so.
2. Underneath meditation is the simple idea of acceptance.
3. Hustle and grind are useful tools, but they are not useful in every situation. Consider adding meditation to your repertoire.

12

Belief and Faith

"Fear believes in a negative future. Faith believes in a positive future. So if neither has happened yet, why wouldn't you choose to believe in the positive future?"

—*Jon Gordon,* New York Times *Best-Selling Author*

Belief and faith go hand-in-hand with risk. If risk is on the tactical side of the equation, involving real-world choices and operations, belief and faith are on the spiritual and philosophical side. You may not need to have faith or belief that your light will reach others if you're going to keep it hidden under your own little bushel—but what kind of a life is that? Cramped and lonely, with no room for growth, such a life would not be very fulfilling. It might be safe from the potential dangers of the world, but at what cost? If you never take the leap, there is no chance that you will fly. But if you do have the courage to take the leap, you will need a healthy dose of belief in yourself, for doing all of the things described in this book, and faith in the world beyond you, that it will support you and provide the wind beneath your wings so you don't crash upon the shore below.

Don't Be the Guy (or Gal) Who Woke Up on Third Base Thinking He Hit a Triple

A good path to believing in yourself is finding a way to believe in the world around you. This can be a challenge if you were mistreated or abused or grew up with very little. By acknowledging that the world has already supported you, even with very little evidence that it has, you can grow your faith by embracing the idea that, if you do your part, the world will eventually support your effort. There are some men and women who have pulled themselves up by their own bootstraps and they deserve our respect. It may be hard for them to give in to the "weak" concept of having faith. They don't need faith, the logic goes, because they were prepared on their own. They don't need protection, they say, because they were strong enough to withstand harsh realities. While I completely understand that logic, I believe that even the strongest among our race of imperfect humans got to where they are today because at some point, maybe after massive amounts of effort on their part, they had to start relying on some*thing* or some*one* outside of themselves.

One needs only to experience an earthquake to realize that we are actually employing faith in things we mostly take for granted, like gravity and the ground beneath us, every single day. By logging all of these things that we can already be grateful for *right now*, we can make ourselves more aware of this belief and faith and then *cultivate* more of it. This is a way to increase the chances that it doesn't show up only when the wind blows at exactly the right angle.

"I got to the point where I had everything I thought I ever wanted, but I still didn't feel happy. So I sold my companies and started a new one. The whole point was that I wanted to replace the thought, 'I'll be happier when _____' with the thought, 'I'm happier now, because _____.'"

—*Nataly Kogan, Owner/CEO, Happier, Inc.*

Nataly Kogan, one of my past guests on the *10,000 NOs* podcast, had every reason to believe in herself. When her family came to the United States from Russia she did not speak English. She credits Alyssa Milano and reruns of *Who's the Boss?* for learning the language. Eventually, through inordinate amounts of hard work, she became a successful entrepreneur. But, just as Oprah preaches that happiness comes from gratitude rather than material possessions, Nataly discovered that what was lacking in her life was the acknowledgment that she had plenty to be grateful for right now. She created an entire company and mobile app to encourage herself and others to stop looking for happiness around the next corner.

Create Your Own System for Gratitude

I have never coined a catchy phrase like my guest Charlie "Rocket" Jabaley. His mantra, "I'm on a winning streak," went viral after he convinced the Duke men's basketball team to shout it in unison with him on Instagram the day he delivered a motivational talk to them. Prior to that, he had repeatedly told his followers the mantra can be uttered to celebrate things as trivial as having an espresso made at Starbucks and as monumental as closing a business deal. I did realize, however, that I'd been doing something similar my entire life without being aware of it.

As my kids can gladly tell you, I am annoyingly consistent when it comes to acknowledging beauty around me.

Every time we drive down the California Incline strip of road between the Santa Monica bluffs and the Pacific Coast Highway on our way home, I point at the mountains near Malibu jutting into the Pacific Ocean, "Do you realize how lucky we are? People travel from around the world to see this view!" As would be expected, they show their gratitude for Dad's life lesson with an eye-roll and a shake of the head, but I can't help myself. Likewise, I make a point of telling family and friends how much they mean to me on a regular basis, whether through text, email, or just in a conversation. Try it. What you'll find is that, when things are going horribly wrong in your life and it feels like you can't catch a break, you'll at least have evidence that reinforces the idea that the world is good to you in some way, shape, or form. It will systematically increase your ability to have faith.

Looking back at the skydiving story I shared in the chapter on risk, what allowed my wife and me to experience hurtling through the air toward the earth from 13,000 feet at terminal velocity was an implicit trust in the equipment and the manufacturer's ability to design and create it. Our faith was not just in the ropes, pulleys, and parachutes, but also the plane, the engines, and the pilot. We had to have faith that our guide, Gus Kaminski, and his training and expertise as the captain of the Navy SEAL Leapfrog team would get us to the ground in one piece. In fact, from the minute every one of us wakes up each day, we are placing our faith in hundreds, if not thousands or more, of people who came before us. The reason I can type these words into my computer is the hundreds of thousands of hours of research, trial and error, bloodshed, and hardship that went into its creation, as well as that of every little gadget we take for granted. Life requires a hefty amount of faith in others, both living and deceased. And yet, when we are called upon to have faith in larger areas of our life, we become skeptics and cynics, unable to take chances for fear of getting hurt.

> "He said, 'What do you want to do, Little Heath, when you grow up?' I was like, 'Oh, I'm gonna play in the NFL.' And I remember him looking to my Dad, and this is my first conscious, memorable thought of someone kind of doubting what I felt like God just put in me as a youngster. He said, 'The kid doesn't have a clue how hard it is to make it.' And I was four. How I remember that, I don't know. I think it was that first kind of heart wound of like, 'Oh. You tryin' to squash what I'm dreaming of?'"
>
> *—Heath Evans, 10-year NFL fullback,*
> *Super Bowl Champion*

When I decided to become an actor, with no Plan B, it was faith that kept me from turning back. I had a trust that if I did the work, and had some talent, someone would eventually acknowledge it. It required grit and determination on my part, sure, but all of that would have amounted to nothing if not for the teachers, friends, mentors, and opportunities that I believed would show up to help me. And they did show up. Except when they didn't. And when they didn't, I'd just tell myself it was for a reason I couldn't yet see, and I'd believe they'd show up the next time. Some people hear my stance on this topic and think that it's blind. They're not completely wrong. Remember that phrase I told my wife, "willful denial"? I could also call it "intentional blindness." Having faith requires us to see what we want to believe, even if it's not right in front of us. And while faith is not asking us to ignore what is right in front of us when it is not pleasing, it is saying, "Yes, this may be the case *right now*, and you need to accept it, but that doesn't mean you have to focus on it and make it *worse* than it really is, or that it can't change for the better."

My late cousin David Ferrara, a successful entrepreneur before his premature death, used to say, "If you're not stretching, you're not growing." Morgan Freeman's *Shawshank Redemption* character, Red, whom I quoted in an earlier chapter, famously said, "Get busy living or get busy dying." Either direction, change is occurring all the time. Faith is a belief that that change will not always be against you. Cancelling my bartending shift the night before my *Sopranos* audition was in faith that, against the likely odds, I would at least have a shot at that role. I can't count how many times before and after that audition I have risked from that same premise and lost. But, because I choose to see those losses merely as steps toward my next win, triumph is inevitable.

Why Not Me?

I am aware that the cynics among you think this sounds like complete and utter hogwash. Bad things *do* happen to good people, and great effort is often *not* rewarded while cheating and boisterous behavior many times *are* rewarded. All that being true, my question, like Jon Gordon's, is:

Why believe anything but that which will empower you?

When I failed to score the role in the soap opera after my screen test, would it have been smarter to interpret that as a sign that I had no right to be a professional actor? If I had done that, I never would have auditioned for *The Sopranos* just a short time later. When I was told I was the frontrunner for the role on *The Sopranos*, but at the final callback saw the names of actors from the biggest agencies in the business on the sign-in sheets, would it have been smarter to leave the office and take the subway home? I remember considering that. I had made it this far, but it was ludicrous to think that a show of this stature would ever give this job to me. But the fact is, they did. Sometimes it is you. This is why I often ask myself, "Why *not* me?"

I'll never forget walking down Fifth Avenue about an hour after that final callback, December 20, 2001. I had a message on my phone from casting director Georgianne Walken and it didn't sound good. "Hey, honey … I just wanted to tell you … " her voice sounded somber until, after a brief pause, she uttered the line that changed the course of my career, "You got the part, kiddo!" When I woke up that morning, I didn't know that would be the case. And, likewise, wherever you are right now, *you have no idea where you'll be tomorrow*. None of us does. It could be in the position you've dreamed of for a lifetime, or it could be in a morgue. Sounds morbid, I know, but it's that razor's edge that we straddle every day that gives value to every breath we are lucky enough to breathe above ground. With such limited breaths, why would you choose to believe in anything but your greatest dreams coming true?

Losing the Battle but Winning the War

Rather than just share an example of where belief and behavior led to a win, I want to share a story of one of my *10,000 NOs* guests, Rob Whitaker, who was battling cancer when we sat down to talk, a battle that, sadly, he eventually lost. Whitaker had every reason to complain and be a victim: at age 43 he went in for a typical annual physical and just a few days later, completely out of the blue, was told by a doctor that he should "get his affairs in order." Rob was diagnosed with Stage IV colon cancer. He could easily have rolled over and died right then, but instead he chose to fight his cancer by living his life to the fullest with his wife and children. He also fought it with an irreverent humor not commonly applied to cancer.

"I see a lot of this at Sloan, cancer patients are funny, right? They like to talk and they like to talk to other people with cancer … but they like to talk to people with cancer that are worse than them. Right? It's kind of a f#%ked up hierarchy in there, right? There's, like, ya know, the Freshman and the JVs and the Varsity and then, even to like the Grad guys, ya know? The pro level cancers. And, uh, unfortunately, I'm like pro level cancer."

—*Rob Whitaker, on his fight with Stage IV colon cancer*

Instead of using the hushed and precious tone that is commonly associated with conversations about cancer, Rob would write beautifully crafted, wickedly funny passages that documented his trials and tribulations in bimonthly emails to his family and many friends, titling them "Rob's C-Notes." They were so funny and unique that when my sister-in-law, a friend of Rob's, read them to us one morning after I had just launched my podcast, I said I needed to meet him. By approaching his big "no" with the heart of a warrior, Rob inspired not only his wife and children, who have suffered through his death, but many other cancer patients and their families who face similarly long odds. He is a prime example of how a good attitude and belief in something larger than the challenges in our immediate sight can allow us to win the war for others, even if we lose our own particular battle.

Keep Your Own Scorecard and Start with Easy Wins

Many people defend their lack of expansion by vehemently exclaiming that "you are who you are." But humans are capable of huge change. Even doubters admit they have a capacity for change when it comes to tangible skills. They just don't believe it applies to aspects of life that they consider to be intangible, like belief and faith. These skeptics write off the idea that they can systematically increase their ability to believe in themselves because they mistakenly imagine people like myself proposing a program that consists of repeating a mantra for eight hours a day while not doing anything differently. What I am proposing, however, is more along the lines of Don Saladino's advice in the chapter on transformation: start small at first, and allow your ever-increasing self-belief to grow with each tiny win.

Biting off more than you can chew is a good path to eventually quitting. I've seen too many young actors throw in the towel because they compared themselves to Gary Oldman. The gap between his ability and theirs was so large that the only logical thing to do was quit. While I wholeheartedly believe in striving for greatness and eventually being considered one of the elite, part of the problem with this approach is that it's like an ant weighing itself on an elephant's scale. Had I berated myself for not being nominated for an Oscar for my performance in *The North End*, my first feature film, that would have been insane. Just as NFL great Tom Brady does not berate himself for not hitting as many homeruns as former Major League Baseball star Derek Jeter, because football doesn't allow for homeruns, you need to pull things into your own wheelhouse first. Once you build momentum and gain confidence, then you can recalibrate your scale and start to work toward your next goal. The way one eats an elephant is one bite at a time.

You Don't Need a Scorecard to Know If You Won or Lost

Momentum is a game changer, so you need to cultivate it. My friend Chris Messina and I used to jokingly call ourselves

"The Dali Chrissy" or "The Dali Matty" when we were on a hot streak as actors because, at those times when one of us was employed, our advice to the unemployed counterpart (me or Chris, depending on who was up and who was down) was always, "Just relax … it'll come to you." That's easy to say when things are going your way, but not so easy when you can't get a job if your life depended on it.

For that reason, my friend Blake Robbins and I came up with an approach to scoring our own auditions that did not rely on outside opinions. After reading a book on John Wooden, one of the winningest coaches in college basketball history, I shared one of my takeaways with Robbins. Wooden told his players that when they returned to UCLA on the bus from away games, he did not want their families or girlfriends to know if they won or lost based on their behavior. He believed that too much celebrating after a win, or too much sulking after a loss, meant they had judged their performance by the final score on the scoreboard. In his opinion, the game was won or lost before it was played by the way the team prepared. He was more interested in them "leaving it all on the court." Ironically, when they did that, they usually won on the scoreboard, too. From then on, when Robbins and I would grade our own auditions, we would describe them as a "win" or a "loss" before we found out if we got the job. This was a way to control our own internal barometer and set it for success rather than allowing someone else to turn it way up or down.

Regardless of your field, or what aspect of your life you are dissecting, self-belief and belief in others around you is imperative. Do everything you can to cultivate it and with each small victory you'll be on your way to unlocking a more confident version of yourself. Some of you may view this in religious terms and look to God for your strength. Others may view it in the sense of putting faith in the universe. Still others will view it more pragmatically, based on tangible, measurable accomplishments.

Regardless of the semantics you use, belief and faith come from gratitude for what you have now and what you will eventually gain on your own.

Top Three Takeaways

1. Make a gratitude list of things and people you rely on that are already in your life to build your belief that the world around you will support you.
2. Ask yourself, "Why not me?" Then, when you *do* get the results you were after, be sure to log them so you can draw upon them in the future.
3. Belief and faith may not get you through your current struggle, but by having them, at the very least you leave an inspiring legacy behind.

13

The Subconscious

"While your conscious mind is five horses pulling you in one direction, without your knowing it, your subconscious is like ninety-nine horses pulling you the exact opposite way."

—*Zander Fryer, CEO/Founder,*
Sh*t You Don't Learn in College

Carl Jung is famous for his work with the subconscious. According to Jung, our conscious mind is like a tiny cork bobbing in the sea of our subconscious. If you buy into that image, you begin to understand that gigantic forces from within you, of which you are not fully aware, are swaying your decisions every day.

Dreamwork

My interactions with Jung's work have come mostly through
my study of acting with coach Kim Gillingham and her protégé
Amanda Lovejoy Street. The work we have done together is
commonly referred to as "dreamwork" or "mat work," because
a lot of it is done from a yoga mat, many times with the student
lying on his or her back.

I find it noteworthy that much of dreamwork is done with
the subject on the floor. In many ways, this work is the opposite
of grinding. To envision the difference in the approach, consider the quote that begins this chapter from past *10,000 NOs*
podcast guest Zander Fryer. He said this to me when we began
our work with my subconscious around the area of self-belief.
To untangle this mostly mysterious knot of thoughts, feelings,
and emotions, the practice of dreamwork does not come at it
head-on. Instead, the subconscious is summoned before bedtime
with something like this in a journal that is kept at your bedside:

Dear Inner Self,
    If it is your will, please reveal to me in my dreams
tonight the essence of what you want me to know about
this project. Illuminate me with your creative will. Help
me to see how I can come closer to you through this
creative work.
    And/or ... please reveal to me how my own struggle is
the same as the struggle of the character.
    With my respect and love,
    Me

This particular verbiage was given to me by Amanda
Lovejoy Street as we were preparing for my role on *Goliath*. The

beauty of it is it can be tailored to whatever your situation is, regardless of what you do for a living.

The next step is to go to sleep and when you wake up after a dream, immediately scribble down any details from your dream while trying not to wake up completely. These details do not need to make sense as you write them down. When you go to do the mat work, you are helped into a meditative state and begin to make associations with various aspects of your dream.

> "Why did this role, this script, this project hurtle through the universe and land on your lap right now? What are you going through right now that can inform your character? And what can this character, and this story, teach you about what you're struggling with?"
>
> —*Kim Gillingham, Acting Coach*

The idea is that your subconscious is constantly working out struggles underneath the surface unbeknownst to you. Every night, the subconscious produces a show, which we call a dream. And in representing the various aspects of your whole self, the subconscious will cast people from your life that might include friends, relatives, celebrities, or even pets. These "players" will then present "the show" to you and you'll wake up saying you had a dream. The philosophy of Jung, and his students like Gillingham and Street, is that these dreams can be studied and interpreted so that they can be harnessed in a way that can *help* us, rather than *push* us through our lives like pawns on a giant chessboard.

A Hollywood Nightmare of Self-Sabotage

If this is sounding too much like a mystical sci-fi movie for you to handle, simply ask yourself if you've ever done something that, while you were in the midst of it, you knew was going against what you wanted consciously. I have my own incredibly embarrassing story involving four-time Academy Award–nominated actor Ethan Hawke. It happened on my first day of his 2001 directorial debut, *Chelsea Walls*. To set the stage, you need to know where I was in my career and just how much this gig meant to me to fully understand this story's ranking on the cringe meter. It was pre-*Sopranos* for me, back in the day of bartending and doing black-box theater for free, living in my rent-stabilized fifth-floor walk-up apartment. I got a call from a guy with whom I had gone to preschool but then mostly fallen out of touch. We had reconnected through some mutual friends and it turned out he was now working for Ethan Hawke. Several months after reconnecting, he reached out to me saying he was working with Hawke on his directorial debut and there was a role for which I might be appropriate.

The terms "hurry up and wait" and "feast or famine" are not an exaggeration when it comes to a life in show business. The time between receiving my friend's call while I was sitting at my desk on the Upper East Side and arriving in a casting office's waiting room downtown was probably just over an hour. The lack of prep time called for quick and instinctive choices to be made. The role was not extensive, but there were two scenes in which I saw some opportunity for a little grounded humor and levity. I was auditioning to play a rookie cop who, along with his senior partner, is called to the scene of a suicide in the Chelsea Hotel. Other than the actual material, the simultaneous excitement and stress I possessed came from the fact that I'd be auditioning for Hawke himself, an actor who I had been impressed with since I saw his performance in *Dead Poets Society* when I was in high school.

Unlike any other audition I'd had before or have had since, I never went into this particular audition room alone. I was paired with another actor who, it turned out, was a retired police detective from Long Island. We were told we'd be auditioning together, so we looked through the scene, reading it aloud in the waiting room once or twice, before going in. Hawke couldn't have been kinder, and before we even read the scene, his charm and lack of pretense took away any of the tension caused by his fame. We read through the longer of the two scenes, and when we had finished, Hawke jumped to his feet and high-fived both of us, saying, "That was fantastic!" My scene partner and I left the building together and, despite my being significantly younger than him, my five years of experience made me the veteran. So when he asked my thoughts, I shrugged, "Anything can happen … but I've never had a director jump up and high-five me in the room." We both got the gig shortly thereafter.

> "So, by the time he called me back last, I'll never forget, I just felt so intimidated, I just was like, 'Oh my gosh, this man that I conversed with so easily once upon a time, he's the Godfather of film! What do I say? I'm not good enough to talk to him.' I'm the one who pulled away from that. And then he died a few months later."
> —*Sarah Shahi, Actor, on sabotaging her friendship with her mentor, Robert Altman*

Given the circumstances and my excitement over scoring this role, it's hard to imagine the self-induced nightmare that ensued on my first day of filming. It actually makes me tense to even recall this story 20 years later. I set my alarm early despite a relatively late mid-morning call time. Popping out of bed, I ran to my gym seven blocks away for a good workout to get my blood moving and shake out any nerves. After the workout, I returned home and cooked a hearty enough breakfast that I wouldn't be starving on set. I showered and headed toward the subway. If you've lived in Manhattan for any amount of time, you know that subways are relatively reliable, but also prone to delays. This day was one of those delay days. I stood on the crowded platform, waiting for my train. With each minute that passed, I calculated the risk of trudging back up to the freezing cold street to hail a cab. That could be a battle of its own, to get a cab and then to fight traffic to Chelsea from the Upper East Side. The subway, once it came, usually delivered you to your destination with more speed than a cab. My decision to stay on the platform was full of anxiety, even after my train arrived, as I knew I would need to transfer to a bus to get to the West Side once I made it down to 23rd Street.

By the time I made it to 23rd Street, I was so late that I knew I needed to hail a cab rather than wait for a crosstown bus. I ran up the subway stairs in a panic, skipping two steps at a time. I hustled out to the street and jostled my way into an open taxi, urging the driver to get me to the Chelsea Hotel as quickly as possible. If you've ever had a nightmare where you needed to get to an important meeting but somehow couldn't move, this was the living embodiment of it. Traffic was gridlocked to the point where, after several blocks I overpaid the driver and jumped out to sprint the remaining distance.

When I arrived in the hotel lobby, a production assistant pointed me to where I waited for what seemed like eternity for the archaic elevator to arrive and bring me to the appropriate floor. When the door finally opened, I was faced with my worst fear: Hawke was in the hallway, blocking my scene with the other actor. "Dude! Where've you been?!" Because he's a nice guy, he didn't rip my head off, as I'm sure he wanted to, but I was mortified. Not wanting to slow things down any more than I already had, I jumped right in and did my part. His then-wife, Uma Thurman, was also there as she was one of the leads in the film, further compounding the heightened nightmarish quality of the experience. She, too, was inexplicably kind to me and helped to quell my embarrassment. But, as Julius Caesar said when he led his army across the Rubicon River into Northern Italy, "*Alea iacta est*": the die has been cast. I was past the point of no return ... I had screwed up.

Ultimately, the *Chelsea Walls* shoot turned out to *not* be the disastrous experience I feared that day. Thurman proved to be right when she said, "Don't worry, we're not shooting this for a few more hours." By the time we *did* shoot the scene, as well as my second day's work, Hawke was happy with what I did. We had a laugh over my gaffe at the wrap party, which was a relief, but I have yet to work with him again. Along with bringing back a nervous feeling when I retell it, this story has always stuck with me because it was so out of character with how I conduct myself professionally and what I expect of myself. I suspect that people on that set, if they even noticed, assumed I overslept or partied the night before, and that my mistake was the result of me being a lazy, reckless actor. Instead, I was an actor who cared *so* much that he tried to do too many things to prepare himself and ended up shooting himself in the foot along the way.

Looking back, though, I suspect my subconscious was at play. Perhaps, on some level, it was a fear of success. While this sounds strange, maybe I didn't think I was ready. Or it could have been fear of failure; knowing that my last-minute audition was particularly instinctive, maybe I was worried I couldn't reproduce the same magic that induced a high-five in the audition room. But what I really suspect was at play, because it still lingers within me from time to time even now, is that my actions that day were the result of an underlying resentment toward my own desire to be liked and valued by my business. On the one hand, I was ecstatic that someone like Hawke was not only aware of my existence, but valued my talent. On the other hand, I was someone who had gone through the first twenty-something years of my life, prior to my acting career, with a fair amount of success. Now, even when things went well, a significant part of me that I wasn't even aware of was trying to sabotage my efforts by essentially saying, "You don't need to jump through hoops for this guy. Do your daily workout, eat your breakfast, take care of things the way *you* know how to take care of them ... and *then* go do what this Ethan guy asks of you."

It's incredibly illogical and self-sabotaging, but this kind of inconsistency exists in all of us. There is a power struggle between all of these different parts of ourselves who are vying for center stage. But because this war is being waged on a battleground that we don't even know exists, its repercussions knock us off our course despite an exorbitant amount of effort.

Hopefully, you haven't screwed up as obviously as I did that day, but look for patterns in your past where you've followed a leap forward by taking two unnecessarily dumb steps backward. Two of my past *10,000 NOs* guests, Bedros Keuilian and Suzy Batiz, both of whom had very bumpy rides prior to their massive success, pointed me to one of their mentors, who may as well have been describing my curious actions the morning I walked onto Hawke's set when he wrote the following in his book:

> "Each of us has an inner thermostat setting that determines how much love, success, and creativity we allow ourselves to enjoy. When we exceed our inner thermostat setting, we will often do something to sabotage ourselves, causing us to drop back into the old, familiar zone where we feel secure."
>
> —*Gay Hendricks*, The Big Leap

This book about my 10,000 "no"s is not about the subconscious in particular, so I do not consider this tiny mention of it to be sufficient for you. But hopefully it will spur you to seek out someone who can guide you in the realm of your subconscious, if you are not already doing so. If you picked up this book, you are likely interested in getting somewhere and hoping that some clues here will get you there more easily and efficiently. I'd hate to see you struggle so hard with intensity and effort while leaving out this huge piece of the puzzle. Whether it's by finding someone like Kim Gillingham or Amanda Lovejoy Street to guide you through mat work, or someone who uses writing exercises like Zander Fryer to help you with your self-belief and awareness of your subconscious, find ways to delve deeper into it and you will undoubtedly remove some of the barriers you likely have placed in your own path.

Top Three Takeaways

1. There are alternatives to hustle and grind, but each component is a part of the larger whole and has its place.

2. When you act in a way that feels completely out of alignment with your stated goals, your subconscious may be playing a part.

3. Find a mentor or teacher to help you delve deeper into your subconscious so your hard work is not undermined.

CHAPTER

14

Just Be a Good Person

"Be nice. Show up on time. Know your lines. Ya know, small things like that ... hitting your mark. Those small things also prove to be in people's memories, 'She's a professional. Not only can she do the material but we want to work with her.'"

—*Melissa Ponzio, Actor*, Chicago Fire, Teen Wolf

When you've read *Curious George* to your children as many times as I have, you begin to see a pattern. George is a monkey. He is always very curious and, one way or another, by the middle of each tale he has wandered away from his owner, the Man with the Yellow Hat, and found trouble. Whether George has taken all the books off the shelves of a library or been lost at the top of the Empire State Building because he was following the wrong yellow hat, he has aggravated some authority figure in some way. But just when George is reprimanded by said authority figure and facing the threat of some kind of punishment, a group of people, usually children, will come to his rescue. The plea on George's behalf will undoubtedly point out that George's actions, while not always conventionally smart, have somehow helped the situation despite his not following the rules. At this point, he is praised for his help and reunited with the Man with the Yellow Hat, who has finally tracked him down. George is always forgiven because his heart is in the right place and, quite frankly, people grow to like him for this.

Live the Golden Rule

There is much for us to learn from Curious George. It should be noted that, while George ends up being well-liked and his popularity helps his cause, his actions are never *led* by a desire to be liked. On the contrary, George is absent-mindedly following his bliss. It just so happens that what makes George blissful can also be described as kind-hearted action. He helps kids in a toy store reach toys high on a shelf or helps animals in the woods by reporting fires that he sees from his vantage point atop a tree and using his climbing and swinging skills to dump water on them, ultimately extinguishing them. And while his actions tend to end up being service-oriented, the main quality that saves George in the end of each story is that *people just want him around*.

When I was a young actor in the mid-1990s in New York City, I remember being guided by the only professional actor I knew, Patrick Collins. He was someone I had respected and admired since attending his youth group in my hometown starting in ninth grade. He emphasized the power of being a good person. Anyone with an overabundance of ambition can get caught up in trying to maneuver into a position of advantage. This is particularly true in an industry like show business, where there are so many candidates for so few slots. But what was pointed out to me, which most people fail to recognize, is that a play, film, or television series involves a lot of time being stuck with the same group of people hour after hour, day after day, for months on end. For this reason, while talent and ability are certainly highly valued in any performance-based field, just being a good person can be a shockingly powerful asset. Unfortunately, there are some folks I've met along the way who, knowing this to be true, have cultivated entire personalities aimed at making people like them despite their underlying disingenuous qualities. Some of them have used this to perfection and have far better careers than I do, conniving their way all the way to the top. I don't envy these people because, in my opinion, their false ways will catch up to them and poison any of the joy they are seeking through achievement.

Nice Guys Don't Always Finish Last

I'd like to share a story where "just being a good person" benefited me in a major way in my career. I am aware that many of the topics discussed in this book were at play in this story, particularly preparation and work ethic. I am equally aware that 99 out of 100 times when you are a good person it can go unnoticed while someone else, with less good intentions, may be rewarded. While this can be frustrating, I remind you that the aim is not only to attain your goals, but to respect and like yourself while doing so.

A lot of my work has come from recurring hires. I've worked with people on one show and they, feeling like I did my job well and was a pleasant presence on set, have brought me to another show months or years later. What I'm going to share is one of these stories that, 99 times out of 100, would not have worked out the way it did. Frankly, I was somewhat shocked when it came together so quickly and with such positive consequences for me and my career.

Cathy Sandrich Gelfond was a casting director I had met through auditions, but she had never cast me prior to this experience. Nonetheless, we hit it off when I auditioned for her on many different occasions, prompting her to reach out to my representatives to see if I could help her with a table read she was assembling with Robert De Niro and Jennifer Aniston.

Gelfond called me and, almost apologetically, asked me to read the stage directions. Her apologetic tone was because reading the stage directions in a reading is considered a thankless job. It is one that is only noticed when it goes badly. For me, the opportunity to be in a room with a legend like De Niro far outweighed any potential downside. She sent me the script and I got to work preparing.

Having done many readings of plays and independent films over the years, I have witnessed the person tasked with reading the stage directions completely tanking a reading because they failed to realize *they* needed to be the driving force. With their ego bruised over not being asked to read an actual part, they show up unprepared, underestimating their responsibility, and end up killing the pace and energy. This causes the material to suffer. While there may not have been much of an opportunity for me to personally score in this reading, I thought, "Cathy has given me the opportunity to be around one of the greatest actors of all time; it is my obligation to return the favor by not making her look bad."

> "Linda and Shonda hit it off like crazy, and it's led to the last seventeen years of Linda's life. And Linda casting absolutely everything under the Shonda umbrella."
> —*Jeff Perry, Actor* (Scandal, Grey's Anatomy),
> *on the collaboration between his wife,*
> *Casting Director Linda Lowy, and Shonda Rhimes*

The night before the reading, Gelfond called me to explain how important the stage directions were for this reading, particularly in knowing what to read and what to leave out, in order to let the two stars riff. Essentially, I needed to support them, but stay out of their way. Little did she know, I had spent the better part of two days going through my script with a highlighter, making choices as to what was necessary and what could be skipped over. I assured her I would not let her down.

The following day, I showed up at CAA, the largest agency in town, which reps both De Niro and Aniston, and entered the room. In addition to the two stars, the producers were present. Their last film had just been nominated for six Oscars, among other awards. There were several actors present whom I knew personally and a few I recognized from their work. In my mind, all of their careers were further along than mine, giving me pangs of envy and jealousy. I reminded myself I was a role player on this day and I needed to set my ego aside and be a good soldier to pay Gelfond back for the favor.

The reading began and watching De Niro and Aniston riff with each other was a joy. As with many readings, despite not being hip or sought after, the stage directions ended up being the biggest part. The whole event went well; I hugged Gelfond and said goodbye, assuming that was end of it. On my drive home, Gelfond called and said, "I gotta tell you, the producers pulled me aside and asked, 'Who was the guy that read the stage directions? He was wonderful.'" I laughed, thinking she was busting my chops, but she assured me that she was not. She said I was the only actor they asked about. We had a chuckle over this irony, considering our conversations before the reading, and she thanked me again. Before we got off the phone, she said, "I have another film coming down the pipeline that you might be right for." While it was nice to hear this, I took it at face value given all of the experiences I'd had over the years where good intentions mostly did not lead to actual jobs.

> "A big part of being a producer is being out in the field developing relationships, doing interviews that you feed back for the anchor, sound bites. When you are emotionally invested people pick up on that."
>
> —*Kimi Culp, Documentary Film Producer,*
> *Broadcast Journalist*

Low and behold, about a month later, Gelfond called me in for what was then titled *Don't Mess with Texas*, starring Reese Witherspoon and Sofia Vergara. I felt well-suited for the role, and when, upon reading the whole script, I discovered that the character I was to audition for—who is introduced as though he'll be one of the leads—ends up shot and killed on page 16, I laughed and thought, "Maybe they *won't* give this one to a bigger 'name' than me. I could actually book this." I went in and impressed Gelfond enough with my initial read that I was given a callback. Unfortunately, I happened to be working on a TV show the day my callback was scheduled, so I couldn't go in for the director and producers. They said not to worry, that they would be back after they scouted locations out of town. By the time the producers returned to LA, unbeknownst to me, they had decided they would cast an African American actor in that role.

Even though I had zero chance of being cast in that original role now that the specs had changed, Gelfond lobbied the producers to give me a look after what I had done for her at the table read. She just wanted to get me in front of them. Because I had been working a lot at that time, I was very loose when I went into the room. I felt good about what I did and when I finished my read, the producers asked me to go back out to the waiting room. They wanted me to look at the material for a different character,

Detective Hauser. When I did, I saw a few actors I know who are typically cast in *very* different roles from me. I thought, "Well, I'll do my thing, but the chances of my actually getting this role have got to be *slim*!"

After only a few minutes familiarizing myself with the new material, I went back in and gave them my interpretation of the role. Despite the fact that I was very happy with what I did in the room, I was shocked when I was eventually cast. A few weeks later, I was in New Orleans shooting what eventually became *Hot Pursuit*. After twenty years of acting, that was my first time uttering a word in a big-budget studio film, let alone playing an integral part. While it wasn't the kind of role that could necessarily be a breakout, I was number three on the call sheet, right after Reese Witherspoon and Sofia Vergara.

If you trace it back, I really got the role from a relationship and my willingness to take on a thankless job with gusto. My involvement in that table read months before was the result of going in prepared for Gelfond over the years and being a decent person. You never know who the person is who might help you or which opportunity will end up moving the needle for you, so it's a good idea to treat others as you like to be treated. Regardless of the results, you'll be able to live with yourself. That was one of the lucky stories. Full disclosure: I can probably tell you a thousand other stories like it where I did all the same things but didn't end up with a job. The point is, keep knocking and eventually someone will open the door.

An important part of your journey is finding others who share similar values and interests as well as a level of commitment that is comparable to yours. Sometimes these people will pull you up or push you to be better to reach your potential. Other times, you will be the one pushing and pulling to help them achieve their goals. By acting in a manner that honors your own values, you will attract "your people" while simultaneously repelling those who do not share your worldview. By acting in a way that is kind to others, you will undoubtedly end up the recipient of similar kind acts when you've lost heart or your confidence when things haven't gone your way. Having someone there to remind you of your best intentions serves as medicine that cannot be matched by any other recourse.

Top Three Takeaways

1. Living the Golden Rule (treat others as you would like to be treated) is a recipe for more than just "success." It allows you to like yourself while you succeed.

2. Just because most stories don't end with you getting your "brass ring" does not mean you shouldn't do the right thing.

3. The timing doesn't always play out in your favor (I was unavailable for my original callback), but relationships can sometimes override that.

CHAPTER

15

Focus and Singularity

"Nothing that's worth it *doesn't* take *forever*. And I don't know anyone that I admire, whether they're extreme winners like Michael Jordan or they're, ya know ... even chess prodigies. I don't know anybody I admire who didn't put in those hours of deliberate and deep practice."

—*Bryan Callen, Stand-up Comedian/Actor*

If you think about all of the amazing advancements in human history, every one of them came as the result of an individual, group, or entire society being singularly focused on changing something. Whether it was toppling an enemy nation, breaking a world record, or a giant leap in technology, laser focus and constantly applied pressure is what led to the breakthrough. Even in nature we see signs of this: erosion is the result of millennia of waves crashing repeatedly upon the shore, turning even the hardest rocks into sand. Earthquakes may shock us, but they are the result of consistently high pressure being applied along the fault line between two tectonic plates long before we feel their vibrations. Almost anyone can get lucky and achieve good results once, if the planets align for them, but to be considered one of the greats, at the top of your field, takes an almost inhuman amount of focus and singularity to continually beat the odds and change the game.

To Catch a Rabbit, You Can Only Chase One at a Time

Focus and singularity have dogged me for decades, since I began pursuing my career as an actor. I've always had a certain amount of confusion and pain over this—and perhaps you will identify with it in your own career or maybe a different area of your life—because much of my fate as an actor resided in someone else's hands. Or at least that was the way I saw it. While I believe I entered this profession knowing that hustle and ingenuity could be the difference between eating and starving, I was many times faced with where to focus my hustle. When I speak to younger actors now, unless they are the beneficiary of a large trust fund, their biggest challenge is almost always figuring out how to balance the time and energy they devote to their *art* with the time and energy they devote to putting food on their tables. This is because most actors face a long period of time when they may gain experience and get training, but they are not paid for it. Extreme competition for roles translates to work for a few and unemployment for the many.

"You always think, 'Now I got *that* ... *this* is gonna come!' And then nothing came. And then I was a waiter, and then I worked as an usher and I was just ... I went way deep into debt and was really, really miserable. And I was trying to make movies so I'd rent cameras now, pay for them, on my credit card that was racking up, to write and direct my own shorts. I'd submit them to festivals ... turned down from *every* festival!"

—*Mark O'Brien, Actor* (City on a Hill), *Filmmaker*

Humans, like dogs, are highly motivated by rewards. We have a golden retriever and when he is in our backyard, chewing on a bone or sneakily attempting to dig a hole, it is easiest to get him inside by offering a treat, a reward for his obedience. The question that we all need to ask, however, is which rewards are we seeking, and what are we willing to give up in order to get them? Here we are, back where we started, talking about pleasure and pain. For us to delve deeper, we need to ask ourselves which pain we are willing to endure and know why we are willing to endure it. As I said at the very beginning of this book, that "why" will be the engine that propels us to block out all distractions on our way to mastering our chosen field and possibly even changing it for everyone else who follows.

I have come to realize that most people, unless they have some personal connection to an actor, vastly *over*estimate the amount of glamour in an actor's life. Those same people would be shocked to read the next two stories I'm going to share. I credit these stories as two of the major reasons I am still a professional actor today. I assure you, they are not glamorous in the least. One involves waiting tables. And the other involves the apartment I remained in for seven years to save money.

Esteemed Member of Society : What do you do?
Young Man : (full of hope) I'm an actor.
Esteemed Member of Society : Which restaurant do you
work in?

    If you're the young man in that exchange, as I was, you generally bite your tongue, smile politely, and accept this tradition of hazing like a good sport as you quietly plot your revenge. The "restaurant bit" is, for the most part, accompanied by a wink and intended to be good-natured. But humor, particularly a joke that has passed the test of time, tends to come from an underlying truth. And the truth for me is that I spent a lot more time waiting tables and bartending than I thought I'd have to when I set out on my journey. Despite this fact, I made a decision very early on that I believe foreshadowed my sustainability in my fickle business. This decision had nothing to do with actual acting. It wasn't about choosing one project over another or whether or not I should grow a beard or wear an eye patch for a particular role. It had to do with focus and singularity and I believe it kept me from going down a rabbit hole in which I've seen many others trapped over the years.

To BBQ or Not to BBQ? That Is the Question

When I first arrived in New York City, on January 1, 1995, I hit the pavement looking for a job. I had bounced, bar-backed, and bartended to earn spending money all throughout college in Boston. Despite this, I had never learned how to wait tables until the fall of 1994, when one of my castmates from *The Mystery of Edwin Drood* helped me get a job at a designer pizza restaurant in Stamford, Connecticut. Knowing how important a sideline gig was for an aspiring actor, when I got to NYC

I pulled out as much charm and hustle as I could, on as many applications and interviews as possible. I landed a gig at what was considered to be a very solid restaurant in Midtown, near the theater district. Virgil's BBQ was owned by the same people who owned Carmine's Italian restaurant, and anyone who lived or passed through New York City in the mid-1990s would know that these establishments were slammed with customers on a daily basis. In short, I had hit the bull's-eye.

Like any other microcosm, there was a power structure at Virgil's BBQ. When it comes to restaurants, all shifts are not created equal. Lunch shifts, while very respectable at a busy place like Virgil's, typically do not yield as much money as dinner shifts. On top of that, if you were an actor whose sole purpose in having this job in the first place was to support your "acting habit," lunch shifts often interfered with audition opportunities. All positions in a restaurant, likewise, are not created equal. In many restaurants, tips were pooled among every employee working a particular shift, but a much larger percentage of the pooled tips went to the waitstaff. The bussers and food runners had to get by on significantly reduced earnings. If you recognize this power structure when you enter this environment, you realize that the only way to the top is to perform well and stick around until enough people leave and you are the employee with the most seniority.

Knowing my tendency to be a worker bee, I accepted this challenge. But I noticed something very early on that alarmed me. I was 22 years old, and when the schedules would be assigned, I observed the envy that everyone possessed for those on top of the power triangle. I also observed that many of the staff were in their early 30s. I quickly realized that almost all of my coworkers, who were aspiring actors like me, had been sidetracked. Their focus had become about climbing the Virgil's ladder to the top, where the plum shifts resided. I am so grateful that I somehow recognized this as quickly as I did and, hearing about a new restaurant opening across town from a friend in my acting class, I jumped ship and applied for a new job. I planned to get in on the ground floor and have seniority so I could tailor my work schedule around my acting rather than vice versa.

I still remember the reaction I got from my coworkers at Virgil's, as though I was leaving Harvard to go to study at a community college. But I had remembered what they had forgotten: my goal was to rise through the ranks of show business, not the restaurant business. The initial dip in my income from the less lucrative California Pizza Kitchen was quickly replaced by comparable tips when, being on the team of staff that opened the restaurant, I had seniority. Not only did my schedule benefit, but when they found out I had bartending experience they put me at the counter, which typically made more money than the waitstaff could make from the floor.

My Very Unsexy Manhattan Apartment

While stories of places like California Pizza Kitchen, where I literally wore polyester pants and a tie with waves on it, are not typically what morning talk shows want to hear about when interviewing an actor, I share them because they are useful. My Virgil's-to-CPK shift was a game-changer, as was the fifth-floor walk-up, rent-stabilized, railroad apartment I rented from 1995 until the end of 2002. When I tell you that this apartment will never make it into a photo shoot, please trust me. The apartment's straight floor plan, passing through rooms like you'd pass through cars on a train, is how these apartments earned their "railroad" status. Each room had an exposed radiator under the window as well, so you had to be careful not to scorch yourself by touching them in the winter months.

Many actors I meet nowadays raise their eyebrows when I tell them I lived on the Upper East Side for such a long time because it was not a very hip part of town. But that was the same reason I could find this place for $1,000 per month. Depending what part of the country or world you are from, that may sound like a lot of money, but in New York City, even in the mid-1990s, it was a relative steal. On top of that, it was a corner unit and it wasn't surrounded by high-rises, so it had ample light, which meant a lot to me. The bedroom in the back was larger than most of the other apartments I had seen, even more expensive places. The one problem, however, was that there was only one small closet in the entire unit, near the entrance (lack of closet space is another hallmark of New York City apartments). With all of its shortcomings, I knew this was the place for two reasons: (1) it was rent-stabilized, which meant if I could stomach staying there for a long enough time, its price relative to the rest of the city would be better and better each year as the rent could only be raised a small percentage, and (2) the bedroom was large enough that, with a little vision and elbow grease, I could turn this one-bedroom into a two-bedroom, get a roommate, and split my rent in half.

"You're an actor. Act, motherf***er!!!"

—*Quentin Tarantino*, True Romance

Singularity and focus have a great way of helping us do things we may not think we are capable of initially. Such was the case with this apartment. Leaning on my cousin's advice and instruction as a builder, I figured out how to build a legitimate wall, complete with a real door, to split the bedroom in two. Because I didn't own the unit, I had to be mindful of not damaging the floors when I fastened the wall while still making it strong. Drawing on the design my college roommate and I had used our junior year, I built a loft for my bed, under which I housed my desk in a little "study nook." For my closet, I swiped an old metal file cabinet my father was throwing out from his office, hollowed it out aside from two shelves, rigged a coat closet rod across the inside, and suddenly it was the most unsexy, albeit free, wardrobe storage unit in history.

I believe that the space in which we live should be inspiring, so even as I describe this to you like I lived in a giant garbage compactor (truth be told, I could stand in my room and touch both walls at the same time because it was so narrow), I was constantly doing what I could to make it feel comfy, welcoming, and orderly. Throughout the years, I did things like install a linoleum floor in the kitchen, paint the walls richer colors, and assemble units from IKEA that showed the TV unit as well as could be expected. With a little love, that place brought me tons of great memories. When my first roommate, a friend from college, got engaged and moved out, one of my best friends from high school moved in. We had so many laughs in that place that we still reminisce about it today. Apparently our improvements were somewhat useful because his younger brother took over the lease for a few years after we left. But the most important lesson you can take from unit 5A on East 82nd Street is that the singularity and focus it took to remain there, even when I might have afforded a nicer place, is what bought me the one thing I really needed: time. Like Rocky Balboa, I was staying in the fight long enough to get my shot at the title.

"All That Matters Is That F*ckin' Box"

Toward the end of the fourth season of *The Sopranos*, I was shooting a scene with the late, great James Gandolfini. I have had the fortune of having worked with some legends, and Gandolfini was definitely one of them. His combination of sensitive vulnerability coupled with the potential to snap a person in half like a twig was why his portrayal of Tony Soprano hit the zeitgeist the way it did. Luckily for me, he happened to be a great mentor as well. Not only did he act with me, but he doled out nuggets of gold that I carry with me to this day.

In this particular scene, we had to enter a room at a casino, extremely inebriated, with my character draped around Tony's shoulders for support as he was too drunk to walk on his own. We rehearsed the scene, as is normal, and worked out the blocking. But just as the lights and camera had been set up for our first shot, before the camera began to roll, Gandolfini put his arms straight out to his sides and started spinning around. He stopped and gestured for me to join him, as a way for us both to get dizzy prior to entering the scene. I was only 30 years old at the time, but I was smart enough to know that when Tony Soprano gestures for you to join him, you join him. So there we both were, spinning like madmen, until the director yelled, "*Action!*" Once he did, we entered the scene swaying, plopped onto the couch, and played through, doing our best to regain our balance after the intense dizziness. This technique helped us to really possess the qualities of extreme drunkenness rather than play at them.

We did a few takes like this, spinning before each one. And after three or four times through, not because I was *really* embarrassed, but more in a lame attempt at small talk, I nodded toward the crew and said, "I kinda feel like a jackass spinning like this in front of them." Not one to miss a teaching opportunity, Jim, as we called him, walked over to me and said, "Hey. Don't worry about them." Then he pointed to the matte box that housed the camera and the lens. And in that incredible way that only James Gandolfini could do, he said, "All that matters is that fuckin' box." It was so simple, and yet, it was a lesson of a lifetime: know what your goal is and block out anything and anyone that lessens your chances of achieving it. He knew the people he was serving and they were *not* the people on that set with us that day. He was serving the story, creator David Chase's vision, his character, and the other people represented in the story. He was also serving the people who, in the years that followed, would experience our performances. He was teaching me to keep my eyes on the prize, and reminding me that the comfort of my ego had nothing to do with what I *really* wanted on that set that day.

In the seventh season of *The West Wing*, I was shooting what many actors would consider a quick and inconsequential scene with the late John Spencer, whom I looked up to as the quintessential actor's actor. At this point, Spencer had shot almost 150 episodes of this show, had won an Emmy Award and two Screen Actors Guild Awards, and had been nominated countless times for other awards, including a Golden Globe, for his portrayal of White House Chief of Staff Leo McGarry. While many other actors would have "phoned it in" for a scene like this, Spencer did not. He remained focused on his character and his character's motivations from episode one to the last one he filmed.

As we set up the shot and ran through blocking, Spencer looked around the desk and found a pen with the Presidential Seal inscribed on its side. He excitedly took the pen and placed it inside his breast pocket before walking over to Christopher Misiano, our director for the episode and one of the show's executive producers. Interrupting a conversation Misiano was having with the cinematographer, Spencer excitedly shared, "I'm gonna keep the pen, Chris. I think I'd have it here because Jed gave it to me when ... " he continued with a specific reference to Leo's past relationship with President Jed Bartlett, played by Martin Sheen. Once Spencer had explained it, he tucked the pen back into his breast pocket and returned to moving around the space, preparing for the scene with the spirit of a child on Christmas morning.

This display of passion, and other displays like it that I was so fortunate to witness from my time with John Spencer, exemplifies the power of focus that I am talking about. Whether you build skyscrapers, companies, or children's esteem, your pursuit of doing it better than most will require similar focus and singularity. While you may have a natural aptitude toward your career or hobby of choice, it is foolish to think that it will blossom into the skill of a true craftsperson without steady and deliberate intention. While this focus and singularity inherently involves sacrifice, what you choose to give up now will be outweighed by the gold you find on the far side of your steadfast journey.

Top Three Takeaways

1. Rewards motivate us. But choosing which reward we want is what puts us on the track we need to be on.

2. Behind any origin story is usually something that contributed majorly to one's efforts that is not as sexy as media or publicists would want you to believe.

3. Know whom you serve or who your character is. It may not be the people immediately surrounding you.

CHAPTER
16

Facade versus Reality

"I masked who I was entirely. And I pretended I was someone who I wasn't. And I hid this person whom I am showing you today from the entire world, including the people closest to me in my family. So my wish is that I can encourage others to do this way before I did."
—*Melissa Bernstein, Co-founder/CEO,*
Melissa & Doug Toys

There's a saying that's been made popular over the past few years in this age of social media: don't compare your life to someone else's highlight reel. While this mindset may be trending now, the topic of facade versus reality is something I have been obsessed with from an early age. Likely, this obsession is the result of the optics of my parents' marriage and our family's place in the community. I often say I won the "parent lottery" because my parents are truly incredible people in so many respects. They are honest, caring, hardworking, patient, smart, and loving. Having their guidance and love is one of the luckiest aspects of my life. But their relationship, despite their attempt to keep it going for 29 years, had its issues, like any long marriage. What makes their situation a little different is that, when they decided to separate after my senior year of college, people in our town were shocked by the news. As I've grown older, I have learned not to be shocked by anything because you never know what's really happening behind closed doors. Growing up, however, I developed a keen eye for seeing how people's presentation many times differed from what was really going on.

Don't Believe the Hype

This chasm between facade and reality, in some ways, became even more pronounced as I started to gain some success as an actor. Television and movies have a way of projecting their players in ways that might appear larger than life. People see an actor on the screen in their living room playing cousin to a famous mob boss, or a whip-smart political handler who ends up with an office in the White House, and they tend to project those qualities onto that person if they ever meet them. But, as you've no doubt learned by this point in the book, those moments are merely blips on the radar of my life. In between those highlights exist large gaps of unemployment, constant rejection, and struggle. So after I started to be associated with some shows that were very widely known, I began to notice how strangers would sometimes approach me on the street if they happened to recognize me from a show or film. In fact, that observation planted the seeds for what eventually became the *10,000 NOs* podcast, and now this book. I realized that if people were looking at *me* thinking *my* life was a breeze, *I* must be looking mistakenly at *others* thinking *they* have it easier than they really do. I have since discovered that *everyone* is negotiating some version of this struggle between their facade and their reality.

The more we can merge our inner experience with our outer facade, the more at peace we will be. I am still working on this, but the podcast and this book are big steps in the right direction because in them I've taken my inner life, at least a larger portion than I had previously shared, and begun showing it on my facade. When I was a younger actor, I used to think that this discrepancy was unique to me. I would point out how so many of my characters straddled two different worlds. Cousin Brian Cammarata on *The Sopranos* was caught between his lily-white existence as a naive financial advisor and his being enamored with the darker sides of Tony's lifestyle. My character of Michael Ambruso on *Scandal* was presented as an upstanding graduate student working toward his MBA, until it was revealed that he was selling himself for money as a sex worker in Washington, DC. The list goes on and on. But with the experience of age, and the benefit of the interviews I've done on my podcast, I've come to discover that *everyone* is straddling more than one world in some way. The goal is to be aligned so that all of our desires are pointing in roughly the same direction. That way, we are not constantly fighting ourselves.

Because the point of this book is to make you feel less alone in your own struggles, it is imperative that I express that these issues are not ones that I solved a decade ago and never worry about anymore. As I've said repeatedly, my education and evolution will be endless, because none of us ever really *arrives*. So the next time you watch a red carpet event before the Oscars, or leaf through *Entertainment Weekly* as you make your way up to the cash register at the grocery store, remember this story I'm about to tell you and remind yourself that *no one*, not even the people in fancy suits with screaming fans and photographers surrounding them, has it made 100% of the time.

Beyond the Facade of the Red Carpet

I've already relayed to you an entire story about my long and winding road from a table read to doing a movie with Reese Witherspoon and Sofia Vergara. The following spring, near the end of the post-production phase of the film, we were given the date and location of the *Hot Pursuit* premiere months in advance. In anticipation of the release of this film, which came during my busiest year of work up until that time, which saw me toggling between significant stints on several shows, my reps and I decided it was worth it for me to invest in a publicist prior to the studio film's premiere. The way it works with big publicists is that you sign a retainer for usually a five- to six-month term so they have time to work on getting you press in multiple media, from online mentions to magazine articles and TV talk-show appearances. This retainer can come with a hefty price tag, but as stated in the chapter on risk, playing it safe can sometimes allow opportunities to pass by without being seized.

Because of the murkiness of the publicity business, it can be hard to quantify how far one's money is being stretched in the service of building one's brand. When a good opportunity comes in, it feels worth it. When there are minimal press opportunities it's hard not to second-guess your decision to spend so much money on something so intangible. There was a fair amount of second-guessing for me despite some photo shoots and magazine mentions. But then a chance encounter I'd had with a journalist from the Associated Press a year prior led to a great score. This one interview, which was eventually parsed up and dispersed via multiple large media outlets, was the spark my publicists needed to grow our publicity campaign even further. By the week of the premiere, as I eagerly anticipated being a major part of Witherspoon and Vergara's next big hit, everything felt like it was coming together at last. The publicists even set me up with a stylist who fit me in an incredible suit, which they gave me, and a makeup artist to prep my wife and me for the premiere.

Warner Brothers and MGM, which co-financed the film, had sent a beautiful black Cadillac Escalade to bring us to the historic Grauman's Chinese Theater in Hollywood. The driver would wait for us, and then take us home from the after-party that would take place at the famed poolside bar, Teddy's, in the Roosevelt Hotel. While I'd travelled in style for jobs in the past and accompanied friends in style to *their* premieres, I had never received this kind of treatment myself. But on the way to the premiere, despite the anticipation of what good fortune might be headed our way, I was acutely aware that, even with all of the work I'd done that year, my fee was not large enough to cover all the expenses I'd been taking on. If you're ever in a similar situation, my word of advice is to hold off on mentioning it to your wife until a *different* evening. I can't remember what incited it, but somehow I blurted out my stress over finances during our ride. By the time we reached the theater, I was able to turn it around and remind her of the promise of the film we were about to watch. But just as my wife was asking me if our financial stress would ever end, our driver had pulled up to the press line and come around to open our car door.

Suddenly, I was in a position in which I had seen other actors from afar but had yet to experience for myself. The entire city block was closed off. Photographers along the red carpet were calling my name, and fans behind barricades across Hollywood Boulevard jostled each other to catch a glimpse of Witherspoon and Vergara as well as the other actors who shared the screen with them. It dawned on me that I was one of those actors. This experience crystallized the idea that what you see is not always what you think it is.

I've Finally Made It to That City on a Hill

I am guardedly pleased to share that after over 47 years on this earth, a quarter-century of them spent learning and employing the tactics and beliefs discussed in this book, I have finally landed a coveted series regular role on a show that I love with people I love. Actor acquaintances of mine who are not in my inner circle have been flabbergasted when I tell them that after all this time, aside from one pilot episode in which I was paid as a regular, for all my previous stints on shows I have been paid as a guest. From the outside, it appears as though I "work all the time," and strangers see my financial facade as whatever they project it to be for an actor who has been a part of as many respectable shows as I have. But the reality tells a different story—one of struggle. My wife knows it, my close friends and family know it, and I'm sure my kids have felt it. There have been near misses, shows that seemed like a "sure thing," and balls that just didn't bounce my way.

I have cried on more than one occasion wondering why, if talented people deemed me talented enough to hire me for all these years, I couldn't be paid comparably to other actors in similar positions. Perhaps it was that I was not owning my power and walking away enough. Or maybe it was our decision to live in parts of town that were not the cheapest because we wanted our kids to have a certain experience. Possibly it was just bad luck. Either way, there was a large gap between how I was perceived and how I was paid. But as this book's final draft was in its eleventh hour, the planets aligned in a way that shined on me and my story changed. By the time you're reading this, I will have completed the second season of Showtime's *City on a Hill* with Kevin Bacon and Aldis Hodge (if the pending writer's strike does not thwart it). Not as a guest star, as I did in the first season, but as a part of the core, regular cast. Does that mean my struggle is over? Of course not. There will be new struggles and possibly recurrences of the ones I've already had. But in the face of constant and consistent professional uncertainty, with the help of so many people, I was able to stick it out until my fate changed. I hope that's the case for you as well. I share this news not to boast, but rather to remind you to keep asking, "Why not me?"

The issue of facade versus reality can be used for you or against you. If you're an actor, examining the differences between the facade and the reality of your character will bring you to a rich portrayal that feels authentic. If you're a financial analyst tasked with assessing the merits of a company as you weigh the decision to invest or pass, studying that company's facade versus the reality of its inner workings could be the difference between profit or loss. If you're a coach or teacher and you place too much emphasis on a player or student's facade, you may overestimate their abilities or overlook their talent. And, perhaps the main culprit behind the rising divorce rate in our society is our epidemic of hoping that our potential mate will live up to the hype they've sold us without digging a little deeper to find out.

A major cause of discontent that I see in young actors (or anyone, for that matter) who either give me too much credit for where I am, or look down on me, thinking they'll be much further along when they reach my age, is that they are failing to look deeply at the whole picture. This failure will undoubtedly seep into their work, not allowing them to really get under the skin of the characters they portray. But maybe worse than that is that putting too much stock in everyone else's highlight reel by comparing it to their entire life will sink their self-esteem and render them much less powerful than their potential.

"Stop allowing others to dump their garbage on your lawn and then complaining about the smell."
—*Carrie Wilkerson, Entrepreneur, Author,*
The Barefoot Executive

So don't believe the hype, particularly the hype that is curated on social media by people trying to make you see them the way they wish they really saw themselves. When you feel imperfect, that's because you are. And that's okay. Imperfection is the mark of humanity. As long as you don't let your imperfections stop you from trying and you continue to forge ahead, battling your inevitable 10,000 "no"s, they are nothing to worry about. Instead, consider having the courage to dig them up and expose them for all to see so that you are *celebrated* for them. After all, it is your imperfections that make you unique.

Top Three Takeaways

1. The more we can merge our inner experience with our outer facade, the more at peace we will be.

2. Everyone has *some* chasm between their inner experience and what they present to the world. Rather than feel alone for that, accept it and begin to close the gap.

3. Do not compare your entire life to someone else's highlight reel.

Epilogue

There's a great scene in one of my all-time favorite films, *Swingers*. On its surface, it's about young actors trying to make it in Hollywood, but like all great stories, it's about so much more than that. Jon Favreau's character, Mike, who has been emotionally paralyzed by a breakup with his old girlfriend, has been dragged to Las Vegas by his much less innocent buddy, Trent, played by Vince Vaughn. After a night spent bopping around a few low-end casinos, where Trent has gone to painstaking efforts to get Mike out of his funk, they find themselves back in a trailer park with two women roughly their age as the sun has begun to rise. Trent, the playboy that he is, tells a dazzling story, most of which is probably embellished, but all of which is thoroughly entertaining. The women love his confident style. It seems like the night is about to pay off for the boys when one of the women remarks, "That's a great story." Mike, unable to escape the prison of his own mind while still grappling with his ex-girlfriend's departure from his life, mumbles, "Yeah, we've all got our stories."

He didn't mean to say that out loud, but the girls look over at him expectantly. They don't know what Trent knows: that, like a moth to a flame, Mike is drawn to a victim mentality that's about to torpedo the night and bring Trent down with him. It's an incredibly funny and cringe-worthy scene in a hilarious film, but what makes *Swingers* a movie I'd watch over and over is that, underneath the comedy, it's about something real. The words we choose and the stories we tell, both to ourselves and to the world, have a drastic effect on the outcome of our lives.

We've all got our stories. We tell them to ourselves all day, every day. Without realizing it, we are the authors of our own destiny, doling out instructions to ourselves on who we are and who we might be on a day-by-day, hour-by-hour, minute-by-minute basis. The way I tell my story now is different than it used to be. With the help of mentors, many of whom I met through my *10,000 NOs* podcast, I began to tell my story in the spirit of Joseph Campbell's *The Hero's Journey*. I cast myself as the heroic protagonist who was stumbling his way through life when he heard "the call." And when that call came, after a period of self-doubt and fear, he answered it. Thrusting himself into a new world he knew nothing about, he forced himself to battle demons, both external and internal, on his journey to becoming his best self.

Even being aware of all of this, it was hard to tell my story as a tale of resilience and perseverance knowing that so many people, maybe even you, have undergone far more trauma than I have. But my former guest, Rob Whitaker, who had been through nearly 80 rounds of chemotherapy battling Stage IV colon cancer, changed the way I viewed the worthiness of anyone's story, including my own. When I confessed to Rob that I had no right complaining about anything after hearing his harrowing story, he told me, "You don't need Stage IV cancer ... everybody's got somewhere on that scale, right? And if you think you're at the worst end of your scale? That feels the same as the worst end of my scale, so it's never a comparison." Sadly, Rob passed away after our conversation, but his wisdom lives on. I share it with you so you realize, as I have begun to, that negating yourself is cheating the world of learning from your unique journey.

In fact, one of the points of this book is that, whether you've experienced extreme loss or have made it this far through your life relatively unscathed, you have had to rely on resilience in some way. Cultivating your grit and ability to persevere will serve you.

I hope that reading this book has helped you if you were feeling stuck, discouraged, or overwhelmed. By the time you've reached this epilogue, you've probably realized that I have felt that way myself more times than my ego cares to admit. My journey has taught me, however, that it's not about my ego. It's about my story having a positive impact on others, somehow leaving them feeling just a little less alone than they felt before hearing it. So my advice is to put one foot in front of the other and head in the right direction to keep following your dreams, or to begin following a new dream, if you've been too wracked by fear to make your first move. Whether you're young or old, healthy or sick, there is always an opportunity for growth. And when the world, or that little voice inside your head, starts to chip away at your confidence in an effort to make you throw in the towel, remember the words of Teddy Roosevelt:

It is not the critic who counts. Not the man who points out how the strong man stumbled or where the doer of deeds could have done them better. The credit belongs to the man who is actually in the arena. Whose face is marred by sweat and dust and blood. Who strives valiantly. Who errs and comes short again and again. Who knows the great enthusiasms, the great devotions ... who spends himself in a worthy cause. Who, in the end, if he wins, knows the triumph of high achievement. And, if he fails, at least fails while daring greatly so that his place shall never be among those timid souls who neither know victory or defeat.

My father shared this quote with me in high school when I was too shy to ask a girl to the prom. I wrote it down on a piece of paper, folded it up, and carried it in my wallet for years. Now it's just seared into my brain. It sits among all the other lessons and mantras I've gleaned from all the incredible people I've been lucky enough to learn from: "failure is opportunity," "nobody walks on the hill," and on and on. I'd be honored if you add them to your own arsenal of weapons as you continue to craft your story and share it with the world.

We all have our stories ... what is yours? Go tell it!

Acknowledgments

It is impossible to sum up everyone who must be acknowledged for their contributions to this book, as it is an attempt to collect most of the lessons I've learned in my nearly half a century on this earth. You'll read about many of the people who have helped me along the way, but one of the points of the book is that every person and situation I've encountered has helped me in some way.

That said, I have received an inordinate amount of help from my wife, parents, siblings, cousins, friends, in-laws, teachers, coaches, mentors, colleagues, and representatives, not to mention inspiration from my kids. I am eternally grateful to be the recipient of so much goodwill.

Special thanks to Jon Gordon, who risked his reputation as a bestselling author when he hadn't known me very long, for introducing me to Wiley on gut instinct. And to my old teammate, Dave DiFranco, for introducing me to Jon.

To all of my incredible podcast guests who have so generously and articulately opened up their life stories so the rest of us could live a little better. Thank you for sitting down with me and being so damn honest and inspiring.

To my loyal podcast listeners for taking the time to leave reviews, send emails and direct messages, spread the word, and let me know that the additional pro bono career I threw on my own lap was not for nothing. Knowing that the *10,000 NOs* concept was resonating with people around the world was enough to keep it going, and keeping it going has resulted in this book.

To everyone at Wiley, especially Matt Holt, Jeanenne Ray, Sally Baker, and Peter Knox, thank you for the opportunity to be an author. A singular shout-out to editor Julie Kerr, who suffered through an endless barrage of emails as she helped me, a first-timer, sculpt my stories and those of my guests into the book you are now reading.

To my acting representatives, past and present, for pitching me endlessly and ultimately allowing me to earn a living playing make-believe. Especially Becca, Laura, Marion, and Mark.

For anyone who has hired me, even those gigs that didn't pay. You gave me a chance to hone my craft.

Lastly, an acknowledgment of the downtimes, the "no"s that led to suffering, the defeats and the doubters who fueled my fire to prove them wrong. And to that invisible force of God, the Universe, Mother Nature, the Collective Unconscious, the Creative Forces, for watching over me and preventing me from quitting when quitting would have been the logical choice by throwing me a bone from out of nowhere whenever I was on the verge of collapse, encouraging me to keep on forging ahead.

About the Author

Matthew Del Negro is a professional actor (*City on a Hill, Scandal, The West Wing, The Sopranos*) and podcast host (*10,000 NOs*). Since launching his podcast, on which he sits down with high achievers from all walks of life to discuss their hard-fought journeys to where they are now, Matthew has become one of the faces of perseverance, resilience, and grit. When not acting, he is frequently invited to deliver keynote speeches on these subjects as they pertain to his rollercoaster journey as an actor and his time as an NCAA Division I athlete. Follow him on Instagram @mattydel or visit MatthewDelNegro.com or 10000nos.com.

Index

Abdul-Jabbar, Kareem, 143
Accountability, 118
  importance, 122–123
Acting
  coaches, work ethic, 15–16
  "habit," support, 181
  lines, memorization (contras),
    21–22
  listening/reading, impact, 73
  origin, 6
  path, *Sopranos* (impact), 75
  roles, transformation
    completion, 111–112
    process, 107–108
Acting career
  pursuit, 7
  sports stories, parallels, 72
Actions
  actors, smallness, 107–109
  lessons, 48
Actors, portrayal, 190
Adaptation, ability, 38
Affleck, Ben, 112
Alex of Venice (Messina), 123
"All Is Lost" moment, 93–97
American Buffalo (Mamet), 109
Aniston, Jennifer, 172, 173
Anxiety, 25
Apartment life, 182–184

Apollo 13 (Howard), 67
Art, creation, 81
Associations, focus, 95
As the World Turns, 73
Athletic performers, artistic
    performers (similarities),
    26–30
Auditions, 162–164
  experience, 8–11
  fear, 19
  increase, 144
  nerves, control, 29
  results, absence, 98

Bacon, Kevin, 195
Bait-and-switch, 82
Bale, Christian, 27, 43, 107
Ballantyne, Craig, 41
Bandler, Richard, 142
Batiz, Suzy, 89, 93, 166
BBQ, usage (decision making),
    180–182
Belief, 116, 147
  self-belief, path, 148–149
Benz, Julie, 32
Bernstein, Melissa, 189
Beyoncé, 53
Blank, Jessica, 1
Blauer, Tony, 17, 37

Bluefishing: The Art of Making Things Happen (Sims), 68
Boyle, Mike, 95
Brady, Tom, 134, 155
Brand (building), money (stretching), 192–194
Brando, Marlon, 38
Breakdown, experience, 7–8
Breakthroughs, 6–7
Bronx Tale, A (De Niro), 23
Bryant, Kobe, 142–143
Budden, Amy, 134
"Burning the boats" principle, 54–55
Burns, Chris, 124–125
Burns, Christopher J., 27, 62
Butler, Gerard, 53

Caddyshack, 134
Callen, Bryan, 177
Campbell, Jessi, 31
Cancer, Whitaker observations, 154
Canvas, content/imagery (reframing/importance), 78–82
Capalbo, Jim, 69
Career
  acting career, 7, 72
  change, 62
  chase, 178–180
  compilation/creation, 109–112
  perspective, 56
  pursuit, 7
  rise/fall, example, 59–63
Caterpillar, transformation, 104–107
Change
  fear, cessation, 104–105
  positive change, capability, 105
Chase, Chevy, 133
Chase, David, 186

Chelsea Walls (Hawke), 162–165
Chicago Fire, 110
Childhood, pain/rejection/loss, 2–3
Choices, making, 49–50
City on a Hill, 84, 110, 195
Collins, Patrick, 171
Communication, 118
  absence, 126
  importance, 121–122
Competitive spirt, presence, 43
Confidence, gaining, 155
Conquest (metaphor), 54–57
Cordial, 53
Cortés, Hernán, 54
Course/path, control, 33–34
Culp, Kimi, 174
Cure, discovery, 99–101
Curious George, 169–170
Curry, Steph, 17, 134

Darabont, Frank, 95–96
Davis, Paige, 127
Dead Poets Society, 162
Death (metaphor), 54–57
Defeat
  admission, 90–91
  surrender, association, 90
Delegation, 125–129
Denial, definition, 81
De Niro, Robert, 23, 172, 173
Destiny, determination, 80
Discipline, 41
  loss, problem, 42
  power, 49
  regimen, 42
  requirement, 45–46, 51–52
Discomfort, lessening, 99
Discontent, cause, 195
Don't Mess with Texas, 174
Dreamwork, 160–161
Duplass, Mark, 16

Eastern philosophies, Western bias, 141
Education, continuation, 191–192
Ego, stardom (relationship), 129–131
Elmaleh, Gad, 29, 46
Empowerment, belief, 152–153
Enter the Dragon, 90
Entrepreneurship, success, 14–15
Evans, Heath, 117, 151
Evolution, continuation, 191–192
Excellence, pursuit, 43
Experiences
adverse effects, 86–87
framing process, importance, 77–78
usage, 100
Expert, listening, 44–45
External experience, 94
External validation, 144

Facade, 5
reality, contrast, 189
Failure
game component, 75
option, absence, 67
risk, avoidance, 55
self-berating, 72
success, relationship, 59–60
Faith, 147–148
requirement, 150–151
Fame, perspective, 56
Fear
impact, 144
understanding, 17–18
usage, 85–86
West Wing experience, 18–22
Ferrara, David, 152
Ferruggia, Jay, 46–48, 50, 108
Fighting, art, 90–93
Finances, stress, 193

Fishman, Roger, 61
Focus, 177
Forces, susceptibility, 145
Fosse/Verdon, 108
Fraturday, 130
Freeman, Morgan, 95–96, 152
Frogs into Princes (Bandler/Grinder), 142
Frustration, 71–72
Fryer, Zander, 159, 160, 167
Fulfillment, gold, 2

Game
failure, component, 75
returning, 71
winning/losing, 41–43
Gandolfini, James (acting approach), 130, 184–185
Garofalo, Janeane, 21
Gelfond Cathy Sandrich, 172–175
Generosity, 130
Giant Steps (Abdul-Jabbar), 143
Gillingham, Kim, 111, 140, 160–161, 167
Glamour, overestimation, 179
Goal
achievement/knowledge, 184–187
grasping, problem, 79
Golden Rule, usage, 170–171
Goliath, 97, 110, 114, 121
Goodman, Elissa, 127
Goodness, 169
benefits, 171–176
power, 170–171
Gordon, Jon, 147, 152
Gratitude
display, 150
system, creation, 149–152
Graves, Alex, 22
Greco, Loretta, 2

Grinder, John, 142
Grounding, exercise, 137–139
Grupe, Rob, 74–75
Gut, trust, 36–39
"Guy in the Glass, The"
    (Wimbrow), 16

Hagen, Uta, 35
Harbinger, Jordan, 127
Harris, Ed, 67
Hawke, Ethan, 162–166
Headspace, 135
Help/assistance, search, 125–129,
    140–145
Helplessness, 70
Hendricks, Gay, 166
Hill (metaphor), climbing, 20–23
Hit shows, occurrence, 34–36
Hodge, Aldis, 195
Hollis, Sue, 145
Hot Pursuit, 83, 130, 175, 192
Howard, Ron, 67
Huge in France (Netflix show),
    45–46, 48, 84, 99, 108
Hughes, John, 26
Humility, 124–125
Hurley, John, 20, 22, 66
    mantras, 69
    teachings, 68

Imagery, reframing/importance,
    78–82
Imperfections, 51
Informational, transformational
    (contrast), 44
Inner self, correspondence, 160
Instinct, 25
    learning, 38
    trust, 36–39
Intelligence, 27–28

Intentional blindness, 151
Internal experience, 94
Introversion, 27–28

Jabaley, Charlie, 84, 103, 149–150
Jackman, Hugh, 105
Jam, Jimmy, 13
Jay-Z, 53
Jeter, Derek, 155
Joel, Billy, 100
    music, usage/need, 8–11
Jordan, Michael, 43
Jung, Carl, 159, 161

Kaminski, Gus, 61–62, 150
Kane, Steven, 125
Kaufman, Boris, 115
Kazan, Elia, 38
Keep It Simple, Stupid (KISS), 2
Keuilian, Bedros, 14, 123, 166
Knickerbocker, Terry, 15, 108
Kogan, Nataly, 149

Lambert, Jack, 143
Lazar, Sara, 141
Leaders
    differences, 131
    problems, 128
Leadership, 117, 127–128
    communication style, 121
    humility, 124–125
    potential, awareness, 125
    relationships, presence, 118
    self-leadership, 125
Lee, Bruce, 90
Levine, Alison, 43, 55–56
Life
    aspect, dissection, 156–167
    change, 73–74

events, framing/interpretation
    (impact), 80
experiences, framing process
    (importance), 77–78
faith, requirement, 150–151
glamour, overestimation, 179
impact, 70–72
perspective, 56
quality, performance
    (correlation), 26
Lindley, Siri, 53, 69
Listening, importance, 73
Live by Night, 112
Lively, Blake, 105, 106
Live performance, spontaneity
    (addiction), 28–29
Live theater, disaster (potential), 31
Living space, inspiration, 182–184
Long Day's Journey into Night
    (O'Neill), 115
Long, Matt, 71, 91–93
Long Run, The (Long), 71, 92
Losing/winning, 153–154
    scorecard, usage (avoidance),
        155–157
Luck, 178, 194
Lumet, Sidney, 114–115, 121

Maguire, Jerry, 126–127
Making Movies (Lumet), 114, 121
Mamet, David, 29, 109
Medicine, usage, 99–101
Meditation, 133
    acceptance, 141
    grounding exercise, 137–139
    integration, 143
    practices, beauty/curse, 145
    resistance, 135
    surrender, contrast, 89–90
Mental game, usage, 41–43

Mentors, study, 43–44
Messina, Chris, 42, 109, 112, 123,
    126, 155–156
Milano, Alyssa, 82, 149
Mindset, impact, 16
Misiano, Christopher, 186
Mistresses, 82–83
Momentum, building, 155
"More than Half of Actors Are
    Under Poverty Line"
    (Vincent), 66
Morski, Lynn Marie, 90–91
Moving, self-questioning, 2–8
Mystery of Edwin Drood, 180
    audition experience, 8–11

Nature, nurture (contrast),
    14–17
Navarro, José, 115
North End, The, 155

O'Brien, Mark, 179
Oldman, Gary, 107, 155
Olsen, Eric Christian, 25
O'Neill, Eugene, 115
On the Edge (Levine), 43, 55
On the Waterfront, 38
Oppenheim, Geri, 114
Opportunity, pursuit (continuation),
    175

Pain, impact, 91
Panic attacks, 5, 94
Parents, impact, 189–190
Participation, requirement, 4
Paskowtiz, Nina, 114
Passion
    display, 187
    importance, 86
Peacekeeping, price, 3

Performance, 25
  audience intimacy, intimidation,
    30
  commonality, 28
  life, quality (correlation), 26
  live performance, spontaneity
    (addiction), 28–29
  magic, 27
  problems, 33–36, 140
Performers
  exposure, desire, 10–11
  similarities, 26–30
Permanent defeat, admission, 90–91
Perry, Jeff, 172
Perry, Matthew, 19
Perseverance, 65, 71
  usage, 66–69
Podcast, initiation, 84–87
Polk, Andrew, 31, 35
Polo, Teri, 21
Ponzio, Melissa, 23, 169
PooPourri (Batiz), 93
Positive change, capability, 105
Power structure, 181–182
Preparation, importance, 21, 47
Pressfield, Stephen, 2
Professionalism, 57–59
Professionals, study, 43–44
Publicity, understanding, 192–193
Purpose, importance, 86

Rarefied air, 112–116
Reading
  lines, importance, 73
  opportunity, 172
Reality, facade (contrast), 189
Red carpet
  attention-seeking stereotype,
    respect (absence), 27
  facade, 192–194
Redman, Jason, 6, 92, 93

Reframing, 77
Regret, feeling, 96
Rehabilitation, meaning, 96
Rehearsal, discipline, 42
Rejections, change, 85–86
Relationships
  change, 134–136
  presence, 118
Relaxation, 133
  integration, 143
  surrender, contrast, 89–90
Rewards, motivation, 179
Reynolds, Ryan, 105
Rhimes, Shonda, 85, 129
Risk, 53
Robbins, Blake, 156
Robbins, Tony, 32, 53
Rockwell, Sam, 108–109
Role models, study, 43–44
Roles, transformation
  completion, 111–112
  process, 107–111
Roles, variety, 110

Sadness, 71–72
Saint, Eva Marie, 38
Saladino, Don, 105–107, 155
Scandal, 84–85, 113–114, 129, 191
Schiff, Richard, 7–8
Schreiber, Liev, 105
Schreiber, Terry, 31, 136–137, 140
Scorecard
  usage, absence, 155–157
Scorecard, keeping, 154–155
Secrets, carrying, 3
Self-belief, 156–157
  growth, 155
  path, 148–149
Self-criticism, 144–145
  impact, 11
Self-development, 127

Self-forgiveness, 110–111
Self-judgment, impact, 11
Self-knowledge, 142–143
Self-leadership, 125
Self-motivation, 4
Self-sabotage, Hollywood
      nightmare, 161–167
Self-scorecard, keeping, 154–155
Service
   importance, 86
   value, 118–123
Shahi, Sarah, 77, 163
Shawshank Redemption, The
      (Darabont), 95–96, 152
Sheen, Martin, 186
Sheridan, Taylor, 113
Show business
   "feast or famine," 162
   "hurry up and wait," 162
   importance/enjoyment, 82–84
Shows, hits (presence), 34–36
Simon, Carly (stage fright), 32
Sims, Steve, 68
Singularity, 177
Skydiving (free-falling), experience,
      60–63
Smits, Jimmy, 18, 20, 21, 129–130
Solutions, discovery, 140–145
Sopranos, The, 110, 162, 191
   acting run, 18
   attention, 59
   audition, 56, 58, 152
   career, changes, 62, 75
   cultural importance, 56
   experience, 22
   Gandolfini, acting approach, 130,
      184–185
   role, callbacks, 75
   success, change, 143
   work, 58–59
Sorkin, Aaron, 19, 20

Speed, purchase, 43–45
Speed-the-Plow (Mamet), 29–30,
      34–36
   performance, problems
      (example), 35–36
   preparation, fundamentals, 30–31
Spencer, John, 186–187
Sports stories, acting career
      (parallels), 72
Springsteen, Bruce (concert
      lengths), 32
Srivatsaa, Sharran, 44, 120
Stage directions, importance, 173
Stardom, ego (relationship),
      129–131
Stars, generosity, 130
Straight-A student, rating excess,
      136–140
Streep, Meryl, 27, 43
Street, Amanda Lovejoy, 160, 161,
      167
Subconscious, 159, 166
   summoning, 160–161
Success
   external validation, 144
   facade, 192–194
   failure, relationship, 59–60
   hype, disbelief, 190–192
   imminence, 72–76
   reasons, differentiation, 80
   simplicity, 140–145
Surrender, 89, 98
   acknowledgment, 92
   relaxation/meditation, contrast,
      89–90
   weakness/defeat, association, 90
System, creation/usage, 49–52

Talent
   impact, 22
   payoff, 194–196

Talent (*continued*)
  payscale, correlation, 194–195
  presence, 112–116
  work ethic/values, connection, 23
Talk the talk, 45–49
Tarantino, Quentin, 183
Taylor, Chip, 37
TB12 method, 134
Teles Properties, 44, 120
Thornton, Billy Bob, 97
Three Billboards in Ebbing, Missouri,
  108
Thurman, Uma, 164–165
Tier One Operators, training,
  17–18
Time, energy (balance), 178
Todd, Jennifer, 123
Torres, Toni, 80
Training, 41
  continuation, 106
  power, 49
Transformation, 103. *See* Roles
  example, 113–114
  impact, 104–107
  initiation, 116
Trilling, Lawrence, 121–122
Truth, moment, 10

Unemployment
  impact, 97
  opportunities, 84–87
Unleash the Power Within
  (Robbins), 32, 53

Values, talent (connection), 23
Vergara, Sofia, 174–175, 192–194
Vice, 108
Vincent, Alice, 66
Vincent, Frank, 57

Walken, Georgianne, 58–59
Walker, Acacia, 119

Walk the walk, 45–49
Walls, punching (avoidance), 97–99
War of Art, The (Pressfield), 2
Washington, Kerry, 85, 129
Weakness, surrender (association),
  90
Wells, John, 20
West Wing, The (experience/fear),
  18–22, 186
Whitaker, Rob, 127–128, 141,
  153–154
Whitford, Bradley, 21
Who's the Boss?, 149
Wilkerson, Carrie, 196
Willful, definition, 81
Willful denial, 80–83, 151
Wimbrow, Dale, 16
Wind River, 110, 113
Winfrey, Oprah, 14, 149
Winkler, Henry, 133
Wins. *See* Losing/winning
  scorecard, usage (avoidance),
    155–157
  usage, 154–155
Witherspoon, Reese, 130, 174–175,
  192–194
Wooden, John, 156
Work
  power structure, 181–182
  recurrence, 171
Work ethic, 13–14, 27
  detail/consistency, 17
  increase, 16
  learning/training, 15
  talent, connection, 23
  usage, 21
Workplace, leaders (problems), 128
World, belief, 148–149
Writing, origin, 6

Yalof, Schwartz, Suze, 142